Useless
Knowledge
for the World
Traveler

555
Curious Facts,
Trivia, and
Misconceptions
That You
Should Know

KLAUS VIEDEBANTT

SCHIFFER
PUBLISHING

4880 Lower Valley Road • Atglen, PA 19310

CONTENTS

A signpost in Samoa shows the islands' visitors that they are rather far from home (nos. 462–466).

Everywhere is life is how German poet Joachim Ringelnatz began his most famous poem. Ringelnatz was right: there is something wonderful to marvel at everywhere, even close to home. For example, in Ringelnatz's own home of Germany, Saxony-Anhalt is the home to a cheesy delicacy that is created thanks to the digestion process of mites.

On a Greek island, tourists do well to take cover at Easter, because the congregations of two Orthodox churches fire homemade rockets at each other. And the building angling for a world record can be found in Abu Dhabi, where the world's most leaning building has an 18-degree angle. Sorry, Pisa, the slant of your Leaning Tower is just 4 degrees.

"Everywhere is life" … and one of the most beautiful manifestations of life is undoubtedly kissing, particularly when the kiss guarantees you fifteen years of bliss in love, provided that you canoodle on "Kissing Allee" in Guanajuato, Mexico. And after fifteen years, you can return to do it again; besides, the city—with its world heritage status—is worth the trip even without giving your lips a workout. Meanwhile, at the Gare du Nord railway station in Paris, kissing is banned completely!

Our planet has a wealth of curiosities and surprises, and some surprises can become downright embarrassing—especially when it comes to social conventions. Over the following pages we have provided a scattering of precautionary tips to help you "not slip up." We also provide suggestions for unusual customs, celebrations, and holidays you can celebrate throughout the year with no reservations—and, frankly, with our encouragement. For example, learn about why the church bells stay sweetly silent at Easter in France or why a foot is a good omen for the new year in Scotland.

Welcome to the Wonderland World Tour!

Klaus Viedebantt

On May 1, Finnish students celebrate Vappu, Walpurgis Night, which begins the night before (no. 36).

1 POPPING UP LIKE MUSHROOMS

Albania. Albania's best-known attraction is a bizarre legacy from its dictator Enver Hoxha (1908–1985). He was dead certain that his country would be conquered by foreign powers, so he had small mushroom-like bunkers built everywhere. If danger arose, each "mushroom" would shelter four Albanians—meaning they needed a total of 750,000 bunkers. However, "only" 200,000 were built, and they are now blotting the beautiful landscape.

2 EASTER TRADITIONS

Macedonia. For the Orthodox Church in Macedonia, Easter, alongside Christmas, is the most significant celebration. Red eggs symbolize the blood of Christ. The first three eggs that the housewives dye before sunrise on Maundy Thursday are the most important. The first one is dedicated to Jesus and placed at the front door, facing the rising sun. On Saturday, all families bring their eggs to the midnight mass, and when the bells chime at twelve o'clock, the congregation calls out, "Christ is risen." Afterward, the eggs are cracked.

3 OPEN DAYS

Vevcani. The village of Vevcani in Macedonia holds a carnival celebration at the end of the year between January 12 and 14 (as per the Julian calendar). The villagers wear homemade masks to drive out all that was evil from the previous year. In many houses, it is still the custom to welcome everyone during the carnival. At the end of the celebrations, the majority of the masks are burned together—which is a guarantee that the new year will be good.

4 ISLET OF STONES

Gospa od Škrpjela. Even in Montenegro, belief can only metaphorically move mountains, but it has created an island: Gospa od Škrpjela (Our Lady of the Rocks) in the Bay of Kotor. For some time, fishermen and sailors, happy to return after long periods away, have been depositing stones in honor of the Mother of God. Ultimately, these stones created an island, upon which a church now stands. Every year on July 22, inhabitants and tourists sail out and sink more rocks.

5 PRETTY SILLY

Belgrade. Belgradians have their own "Silicon Valley." This nick name has been given to a part of the old town that is home to lots of cafés and bars, because you can often spot young women who have been "enlarged" with the help of plastic surgeons. Jokers also like spelling the quarter's name as "Sillycon Valley," with a nod to the English word *silly*.

6 WHERE THE POPE AND PRESIDENT RULE

Andorra. Most people connect this region of the Pyrenees only with winter sports or cheap, tax-free shopping. But few know that this microstate is ruled jointly by the president of France and the bishop of Urgell. Essentially, both of them have only ceremonial functions, but because the bishop, just like all his colleagues, is appointed by the pope himself, Andorra is a coprincipality according to its constitution.

7 TROUBLE IN (TAX) PARADISE

Liechtenstein. With the exception of Uzbekistan, the principality of Liechtenstein is the only country in Europe both without access to the coast and also surrounded by countries that do not have a coastline: Austria and Switzerland. It is like being in a safe, and the country is also used as such. In Liechtenstein, people have stashed billions of euros, dollars, and pounds away from the prying claws of the tax authorities. But times change. Recently, the German tax authority has started collecting in Liechtenstein.

8 GOD SAVE THE FÜRST (PRINCE)

Liechtenstein. British tourists feel very much at home at official celebrations here. The national anthem of the principality sounds very much like "God Save the Queen." Josef Frommelt did not even deny it when, in 1983, he presented his composition to the principality. He based it on an old song from the region, whose melody may have been brought over from England by Liechtensteiners.

9 A SECOND "SERENISSIMA"

San Marino. The fifth of the European microstates is rightly proud of its title as the "oldest active republic in the world." The small mountainous country, an inconspicuous enclave in Italy whose official language is also Italian, is situated close to the Adriatic resort of Rimini. Furthermore, it can point to one of the oldest constitutions in the world, dating back to the year 1600. And, just like Venice, which was also once a republic, San Marino is also known under its honorary title of "La Serenissima," meaning the most serene.

10 TASTY TOWERS

San Marino. The three towers on the Guaita fortress on Monte Titano are not only the landmark of San Marino but also the namesake of the Torta Tre Monti. The "three peaks wafer cake" is the culinary signature dish of the miniature republic. It is made by spreading chocolate and hazelnut cream between layers of round wafers—all topped off with a layer of chocolate. Yum!

11 THE SECRET OF THE FRIES

Belgium. What unites factious Belgium? Chocolate, beer, and fries, of course. The fries are world famous for good reason, because the potato fries, hand-cut if possible, are fried twice. "Soft on the inside, crunchy on the outside" is the motto. The national dish is already protected by law, and the Belgians are seeking world heritage status for them. Incidentally, many cooks historically prepared this delicacy in horse fat.

12 IN ESPERANTO COUNTRY

Amikejo. Esperanto was created in 1887 to be a universal second language for international communication. The first Esperanto state was to be established in 1900 in the German-speaking region of Belgium. Its name, Amikejo, means the "place of friendship." The 2.11-square-mile (3.4 square kilometer) strip of land close to Moresnet had been disputed between the Netherlands and Prussia and was therefore neutral. In the end, the plan for Amikejo did not work out, but Esperanto fans still go on pilgrimages to the region, where there are language courses and restaurants offering menus in Esperanto.

Regarding their national dish, Belgians are in agreement: fries should be fried twice (no. 11).

13 FISH IN RED WINE

Geraardsbergen. Fish and wine make a good combination. But even when the fish is still alive in the red wine? At least that is what the Belgians in Geraardsbergen think as they wash down the small *grondlinge* fish at the "Krakelingen" festival on the last Sunday in February. As a result of animal rights campaigns, only twenty people now follow the old custom ("life revitalizing"). But the campaign's objective was to replace the live fish with marzipan fish.

14 INTO BATTLE WEARING A CRAVAT

Steenkerque. In 1692, the Walloon village gained its place not only in the history between the French and the Dutch, but also in the world of fashion. During a surprise attack, the French officers had no time to properly fasten their cravats, so they tucked the ends of the scarves into their buttonholes. This *steinkirk* cravat became popular and stayed in fashion for around fifty years, despite the French defeat.

15 DON'T SLIP UP

If you dine with a Belgian, you should eat everything on your plate; otherwise, it is considered rude, wasteful, and—particularly if you are in their home—as a criticism of the host's cooking skills. It cannot be smoothed over by (more or less obligatory) compliments to the cook. If you receive an invitation to someone's home, flowers are always appreciated as a hostess gift, but be sure to give an uneven number (but not thirteen) and no white chrysanthemums, which are considered to be funeral flowers.

16 GOOD WISHES PINNED ON THE LAPELS

Bulgaria. On March 1, Bulgarians give each other *martenitsi*: red and white woven arm bands or tassels for lapels. They wear them until they see the first stork, the first swallow, or the first tree in blossom. Then they hang the bands on a tree in order to welcome the spring. Red stands for sun, life, and fire, while white means health and longevity.

17 SCENTED-OIL SPRINGS

Rozova dolina. It's best to visit the "Valley of the Roses" in Bulgaria in May or June, because that is when the flowers' scent is strongest. Shortly after, the blooms are harvested and made into rose oil. For just one gram of the scented oil, which is one of the most expensive ingredients in perfume, one thousand white, red, or pink Damascus roses are needed. This Bulgarian valley produces at least 70 percent of the global rose oil harvest.

18 STRONGHOLD OF WISDOM—AND OF AGE

Sofia. Although the Bulgarians sometimes doubt it, their capital city is a stronghold of wisdom. The name of its patron, Saint Sophia, derives from the old Greek word for "wisdom." Furthermore, Sofia is one of the oldest cities in Europe. Archeologists in Sofia discovered a settlement that is over eight thousand years old. Speaking of age, Bulgaria is the oldest country in Europe that has never changed its name.

19 THE OLDEST HOARD OF GOLD IN THE WORLD

Varna. In 1972, excavator operator Raycho Marinov had his five minutes of fame. While operating the machine close to Varna, he discovered a six-thousand-year-old burial site. Archeologists went on to find the oldest gold jewelry hoard in the world, comprising three thousand pieces of fine craftsmanship and, to date, approximately 13 pounds (6 kilograms) of gold.

20 DON'T SLIP UP

It's confusing. Bulgarians shake their heads when they mean "yes" and nod when they mean "no." Fortunately, many of them have gotten used to confused foreigners, so they generally also say *da*, meaning "yes." Also, if a motorist coming toward you flashes their lights, they are not trying to annoy you but warn you: "police ahead." And, if you are invited into somebody's home, never take lilies or chrysanthemums, which are widely frowned upon.

21 INSPECTING YOUR VEHICLE IN DANISH

Denmark. Before starting their *bil* (car) in Denmark, drivers must check not only the brakes, steering, and lights, but also whether there is a person under the vehicle. After all, a drunk may be lying there. And in the same vein, if you get behind the wheel with a blood alcohol content of 0.20 percent or more, then you'll lose not only your license but also your car.

22 SILVER TO GOLD

Bornholm. The inhabitants of the Baltic Sea island call their ability to change silver to gold "Bornholmer alchemy." In fact, in the course of four hours, silver herrings are smoked over glowing alderwood until they become the golden Bornholm specialty. However, due to a lack of herring, there are now only seven smokehouses on the island, and the majority of the smoke ovens are not lit.

23 4 FEET, 7 INCHES OF BREAD

Copenhagen. *Smørrebrød* certainly put Denmark on the culinary world map. The imaginatively topped, open-faced sandwiches are greatly esteemed in the kingdom and enjoyed as a fine lunch. The center of the *smørrebrød* world is the Ida Davidsen restaurant, which opened in 1888 in Copenhagen. Its menu is 4 feet, 7 inches (1.40 meters) long and offers more than 250 different variations.

24 THREE TIMES LOUISE

Louisiana. Denmark's epicenter for modern art is approximately 22 miles (35 kilometers) north of Copenhagen on the coast and is called "Louisiana." The name has nothing to do with the US state that is home to New Orleans. Rather, it comes from the owner of the property, who was honoring his wives. He was married three times, and each wife was named Louise.

25 DON'T SLIP UP

Since the Viking era, the Danes have been true globetrotters. It could be that they imported from Asia the custom of removing shoes at the door. Guests who are invited into Danish homes should check their socks for holes! Incidentally, Danish guests send flowers for the lady of the house a day in advance. And when saying farewell, an emphatic "thank you" is considered polite.

26 HEADLESS PADDLERS

Danube. Between Günzberg and Ulm, a traffic sign warns travelers of "headless paddlers crossing." The so-called headless paddlers themselves need to be alert too, so they don't repeat the mistake of a German tourist who was carrying his boat in the Canadian wilderness and blindly stumbled into a bear! Fortunately, Mr. Petz was able to flee the unusual aggressor before it made him a head shorter.

"Headless paddlers crossing." It's good that the drivers have been warned! Who would want to reckon with a headless paddler when driving (no. 26)?

Kopflose Paddler kreuzen

27 THE SWAMP THAT BECAME THE CAPITAL

Berlin. The capital cities of various countries have found themselves in the occasional (political) mire. However, from a geological point of view, Germany's capital, Berlin, is in fact a bog. In the language of the first settlers, the Slavs, the word *berl* or *birl* simply means "swamp." And in 1542, Berlin's grand boulevard, the Kurfürstendamm, was created as a log road through the swamp.

28 THE LADY OF UNITY

Rüdesheim. The "Germania" statute high above Rüdesheim is one of Germany's most famous monuments and looks out over the Rhine. Built in 1883, it is often said that she has her eye on France, the arch enemy of the day. But that is incorrect: although she is facing south, she is looking east. In Rüdesheim, the Rhine does not flow from south to north but from east to west. The monument commemorates German unification in 1871.

29 YUMMY BUGS

Zeitz-Würchwitz. Mites? Yuck! But hang on, in Saxony-Anhalt people like mites because they help produce unique mite cheese. Seasoned curd is placed in a box of mites, where it matures for at least three months with the help of the excretions from the bugs. It is said that connoisseurs eat the mites with the cheese. Furthermore, Würchwitz has the only mite cheese museum on the planet.

30 DELICIOUS FALL

Munich. The Oktoberfest has one rule: everything is measured in a *Maß* tankard. A *Maß* would normally be a liter of beer. However, in the Oktoberfest tents, it is generally only 0.9 liter—a special rule in Munich. The tankards are popular souvenirs that can be purchased, but they are also often stolen. The police and security are on the lookout and recover up to 150,000 glasses from bags and rucksacks. The consequence? Prosecution! The judges can issue fines, and repeat offenders may even land in jail.

31 EUROPE'S SMALLEST MINORITY

Kolka / Mazirbe. The Livonians in Latvia are considered to be Europe's smallest minority. Only 230 people have registered as Livonian, thirty of whom still speak fluent Livonian. The fishing village of Kolka is their cultural center. The Livonian culture is best experienced on the first weekend in August in Mazirbe, where the Livonians celebrate the end of their Soviet oppression.

32 SUMMER SOLSTICE

Latvia. The summer solstice marks the feast of Saint John, which is celebrated in many parts of the world with bonfires—harking back to pre-Christian times. In Latvia, young people wearing crowns of flowers go from door to door to wish health, blessings, and fertility. The midsummer meal consists of caraway cheese and beer. In the small town of Kuldīga, a strange midsummer tradition has developed: at three o'clock in the morning, naked locals run through the town. They are rewarded with a beer.

33 NO MORE BUGS

Tallinn. Some hotels around the world house museums, usually of the small variety. In 1991, upon the departure of Soviet troops, the Viru Hotel in the Estonian capital of Tallinn inherited an almost fully furnished museum: a hastily vacated KGB listening station on the top floor of the high-rise. The hotel now assures guests that there are no more bugs in any of the rooms.

34 TANKS VERSUS MERCEDES

Vilnius. In Lithuania's capital, tourists are well advised to always park properly, because the mayor started a harsh campaign against the increasingly frequently illegal parking. As part of a warning video released on the internet, he even flattened an illegally parked Mercedes with a tank! But it wasn't as bonkers as it first appeared: the car was used and purchased especially for the video.

35 DON'T SLIP UP

The three small Baltic States of Estonia, Latvia, and Lithuania are very proud of their independence, which they wrested from their Russian neighbors. Talking about Russia is therefore loaded with many emotions, so as a visitor it is wise to avoid it. Estonians, Latvians, and Lithuanians also don't like being confused with each other. Therefore, you should use only the collective term "Balt" when that is what is really meant. In general, residents of the Baltic States are rather reserved, and they don't like speaking of private matters.

36 FINNISH WALPURGIS NIGHT

Helsinki. On May 1, Finnish students really celebrate. Vappu or Walpurgis Night starts the evening before. Half of Finland, whether studying or not, don white school caps. The most prominent wearer of a school cap is the pretty and otherwise naked *Havis Amanda* mermaid statue, which is found at the capital's harbor. Thousands watch as the students wash the mermaid, and afterward there is a mass picnic in Kaivopuisto Park.

37 SWEATING HIGH IN THE AIR

Kolari. Anyone can sweat when walking uphill. But in the Finnish ski region of Ylläs, the cable railway to the 2,356-foot (718-meter) summit also offers a sauna car. There is space for four in the pricey sauna, which can be experienced year-round behind one-way windows.

38 WELL YELLED

Oulu. In 1987, a group of serious men formed the Mieskuoro Huutajat, the "Choir of Yellers." The singers, always sporting black rubber ties, shout their choral work into the audience, often with the help of a megaphone. They have been on world tours but also often perform in their Finnish homeland. Their repertoire includes their arrangement of the national anthem and recitals of European Union legislation, which have been loudly set to music.

39 THE HEAVIER, THE BETTER

Sonkajärvi. Would you carry your own wife in your hands? Not recommended in the wife-carrying world championship held each year at the start of July in Sonkjärvi, Finland. The skillful participants carry women—not necessarily their wives—over their shoulders, with the women's legs pointing forward, as they make their way over an obstacle course. Beer is waiting for the winner, the amount of which is calculated according to his partner's weight.

40 DON'T SLIP UP

For Finns, going in the sauna is natural, and guests are frequently invited to take a sauna. However, the Finns do not have "mixed" saunas apart from family saunas. Otherwise, the saunas are separated according to sex. The notoriously taciturn Finns can generally become chatty when their sauna culture—in particular the post-sauna beer and barbecued sausage—is praised or if you ask them questions about saunas.

41 FLYING SNAILS

Mogueriec. One place to find *Littorina littorea*, in common parlance periwinkles (or sea snails), is the tidal flats of the French region of Brittany. In the fishing village of Mogueriec they can even fly—at least on the second Sunday in July, when *cracher de bigorneau*, or periwinkle spitting, is the main event. The record is 34 feet, 2 inches (10.41 meters). After their flight, the mollusks are returned to the sea.

42 EASTER TRADITIONS

France. The French Easter Bunny is out of work; instead, it is the church bells that bring both dyed and chocolate eggs to the residents of France. But first, the bells must go on a foreign holiday. They do not chime during Easter Week, and the children are told they have traveled to the Vatican City, where they will obtain sweets and presents to bring home.

The heavier the woman, the more beer waiting for the winner of the wife-carrying competition in Sonkajärvi, Finland (no. 39).

43 KISSING PROHIBITED

Paris. At the Gare du Nord, there has supposedly been a ban on kissing since 1910 in order to avoid delayed trains. An even more bizarre explanation of the ban, which is certainly never enforced, maintains that the original rule was supposedly to prevent electric shocks being passed on through kissing. As if lovers need wires to feel electrified . . .

44 THE POLICEMAN FROM SAINT-TROPEZ

Saint-Tropez. Although *Gendarmerie Nationale* is written on the façade of a renovated old building, the police have long since moved to new quarters. However, tourists still continue to make the pilgrimage to the building to take photos: the ghost of France's most famous policeman, the film comedian Louis de Funès, is said to haunt the house.

45 DON'T SLIP UP

Have you been invited into a French home? Please don't be on time. As a rule, French hosts plan an extra thirty minutes to finish their work in the kitchen or in front of the mirror. And the hosts also like to use the extra time to "air" the red wine. Flowers as a hostess gift? Yes, but not chrysanthemums unless it's a funeral.

46 COUNTRY ON TWO CONTINENTS

Georgia. Where is Georgia? On the Black Sea. Correct, but that is only half the answer. Is it in Europe or Asia? Quite simply, yes and yes. The west of the country is in eastern Europe, while the east of the country is in Southwest Asia. However, if you count the Caucasus as Europe, then Georgia is quite clearly a part of Europe. And that is also how Georgians regard themselves. And, incidentally, they do not call their country Georgia, but Sakartvelo.

47 PROMETHEUS, JASON, AND THE ARGONAUTS

Caucasus. The Caucasus Mountains, which form the border to Russia, feature in numerous myths. The most well-known legend is that of Prometheus. In the mountains—incidentally a ski region that the West is still unaware of—Zeus had Prometheus chained up as punishment for stealing the fire from Mount Olympus. And Georgia is also the country where Jason and the Argonauts stole the golden fleece, made famous in Greek mythology, because sheepskin was once used to collect gold dust from water.

48 A VERY OLD VINTAGE

Georgia. *Gaumarjos* means cheers in Georgian. And the residents of Georgia clink glasses proudly in the knowledge that (as far as can be proved) their country is the oldest wine-growing region in the world. Archeologists found evidence there that is thousands of years old, including drinking vessels, that indicates a planned viticulture. In the former Eastern Bloc, Georgian wine was considered a fine drink. Today, there are plans to develop special tourist attractions in the wine-producing areas.

49 TELL ME YOUR NAME

Georgia. In Georgia you can often tell where people come from by looking at their surname. If names end with the syllable *-jo*, they are generally from western or central Georgia. In the eastern mountainous provinces, the final syllable is commonly *-uli* or *-uri*, while in the rest of eastern Georgia, the syllable *-shvili* is widespread. The most famous Georgian came from the central region but was called Dzhugashvili and is better known as Josef Stalin.

50 COUNTING (PEAS) IN GEORGIAN

Georgia. Vigesimal? A word you don't necessarily need to know if you are not a mathematician or historian. The vigesimal system is based on the number twenty, which is similar to the decimal system, which is based on ten. In Georgia, the numbers thirty to ninety-nine use the vigesimal system; for example, thirty-two is expressed as "twenty plus twelve" in Georgian. But if all this math is too complicated for you, you can relax: the majority of Georgians speak English.

51 BATTLING CHURCHES

Chios. Vrontados on the island of Chios is always in the headlines the evening before Greek Orthodox Easter Sunday. The congregations of two churches fire homemade rockets at each other's church while the devout are praying inside. This spectacle is neither without danger nor legal, but the police respect the custom, which is said to go back to the time of the Turkish occupation.

52 NEW YEAR

Greece. As the year draws to an end, there is no shortage of *scilla maritima* onions at the markets. For a special New Year's Day meal? Nope—the plant, which in the ancient world was ascribed healing properties, is hung on many doors for the new year and is said to guarantee a good year. It is also an important New Year's Eve symbol on the Bermuda islands, where at midnight, a golden paper onion glides to the floor from the town hall, a bit like the celebrations in New York City's Times Square. Why? Onions were once the main crop of Bermuda before high finance fed the islands.

53 GREEK "FLOURING"

Galaxidi. Throwing flour, brightly colored flour to be exact, at people looks like great fun. The villagers of Galaxidi order thousands of pounds of flour and a load of food dye each year to color as many fellow villagers as possible (all wearing old clothes and mouth and eye protection). The flour fight occurs on the Monday before Orthodox Lent starts.

54 MEN WITH STONEWARE PHALLI

Tyrnavos. The phallus is highly valued as a fertility symbol in Greek folklore. In particular, on the Monday before Lent, things can get a bit lively at a phallus festival in Tyrnavos. Those who get caught must drink a schnapps from a stoneware penis and then stir spinach soup with it. You can also sit on a phallus throne. The festival in honor of Dionysus was men-only until the 1940s.

The colorful flour fight marks the start of Lent in the Greek village of Galaxidi (no. 53).

55 EASTER TRADITIONS

England. On Maundy Thursday, the British monarch distributes small pouches to poor and deserving members of the church. The purse contains a couple of normal pound coins to buy necessities, as well as four specially minted Maundy Money coins in sterling silver bearing the value of one, two, three, and four pence. The recipients receive as many Maundy pennies as the monarch's age in years. The market value of a full set is between three hundred and four hundred pounds sterling.

56 WHERE SHERLOCK LIVED

London. London's most famous address is 221b Baker Street. The house, where the famous character Sherlock Holmes once lived, is now a private museum honoring the master detective. Holmes, the creation of author Sir Arthur Conan Doyle, receives approximately seventy letters per week, which are delivered by the Royal Mail.

57 PLEASE, NO DYING HERE!

London. The Brits took a vote on the strangest regulations in the United Kingdom. The rule picked as the undisputedly most wacky: It is forbidden to die in the Houses of Parliament, also known as the Palace of Westminster. The deceased would be entitled to a state funeral with all the trimmings.

58 NEW YEAR

Scotland. The Scots call the New Year's celebrations "Hogmanay," and nobody between the Lowlands, Highlands, and islands can say where the word or its many local customs come from. However, "first footing" is widespread. The first person to put their foot over the threshold of a neighbor's or a friend's home is said to bring good luck for the coming year. It is symbolized in the gifts of coal, black bun (a dark fruit cake), or whisky, which is generally given today.

59 THE SHORTEST STREET IN THE WORLD

Wick. It's a myth that the Scots are miserly. But in the case of Ebenezer Place in the town of Wick in northern Scotland, they really did skimp. The "smallest street in the world" measures just 6 feet, 9 inches (2.06 meters). And much to the joy of the Scots, this record has deposed their English rival, Elgin Street in Bacup.

60 DON'T SLIP UP

The scrumptious English breakfast is one of the few international successes of British cuisine. However, you will be met with disapproval if you order it outside England. In Northern Ireland, you get an Ulster fry, while in Wales you start the day with a Welsh breakfast, including cockles and laverbread made of seaweed. And the traditional Scottish breakfast comprises baked beans and black pudding, a type of blood sausage.

61 RECORD HOLDER IN EGG THROWING

Ballinrobe. The Connacht Spring Show in Ballinrobe, Ireland, is a traditional agricultural show with cattle auctions and sheep shearing exhibitions. The highlight of this rural amusement is the World Egg Throwing Championship. The record for the longest throw of a raw hen's egg is 233 feet (71 meters). The discipline is still under the radar of the International Olympic Committee, but sporty yokels of all nations hope it will soon be recognized.

62 A SAINT ON VALENTINE'S DAY

Dublin. The Irish famously celebrate their patron, Saint Patrick, in style on March 17 with Dublin's lively Saint Patrick's Day Parade. However, less well known is a treasure that could liven up gray February: the relics of Saint Valentine rest in the Whitefriar Street Carmelite Church. They were a gift from the pope in 1836.

63 NO ENTRY IN CRINOLINE OR WITH SWORDS

Dublin. Only one door remains of Neal's Music Hall in Dublin's Fishamble Street, where in 1742 Handel himself premiered his *Messiah*. Due to the expected crowds, the women were asked not to wear crinoline skirts, and the men were told to leave their swords at home. The oratorio was a complete success and still is. In spring each year, there is an open-air performance of the piece in front of the door.

64 EUROPE'S BIGGEST SINGLES NIGHT

Lisdoonvarna. Willie Daly is a matchmaker, a traditional marriage broker in the rural tradition. Every September, he holds a bride show lasting several weeks in Lisdoonvarna, which is located close to Ireland's west coast. The event brings together serious spouse-seekers from both sides of the Atlantic. Of course, there is no lack of Guinness and *craic*, or fun, at an event like this.

65 DON'T SLIP UP

Irish pub landlords like to designate their restrooms in the otherwise rarely used Gaelic language. There is certainly no scarcity of jokers among the landlords, who also like to omit the symbols denoting the gender. So foreigners are generally left to guessing *fir* is "woman" and *mna* is "man." Not quite: the other way around is correct, and knowing that can save some embarrassment.

66 WHERE BLACK DEATH BURNS IN THE THROAT

Iceland. Brennivin, better known as "Black Death," does not look entirely appetizing, thanks to its jet-black label. But its repelling appearance has had the exact opposite effect; the strong schnapps (with an ABV of 37.5 percent!) quickly became Iceland's unofficial national drink and is a popular souvenir for tourists.

67 ONE FOOT IN EUROPE AND ONE IN AMERICA

Keflavík. If you want to fly to the US via Iceland, you actually don't have to go any farther than Keflavík, because you are already in America there—at least on a part of the island. In Þingvellir (Thingvellir), where the oldest parliament in the world met for the first time in 930, you can see how the American and Eurasian tectonic plates are drifting apart . . . by a full 7 millimeters per year!

68 WARM FEET EVEN IN WINTER

Reykjavík. You don't need snow- and ice-proof footwear for a winter holiday in Iceland—at least not if you are visiting Reykjavík or Akureyri. In the two most populous cities on the island, the houses are heated with geothermal energy, which—in a second use—is directed under the sidewalks so they do not ice over.

69 A PENIS MUSEUM

Reykjavík. The national museum, art center, glacier museum, and even a turf church museum—in Iceland there really is no lack of interesting collections. However, the most well-known museum is the Icelandic Phallological Museum in Reykjavík, which since 1997 has preserved and displayed penises from all kinds of animals. In 2011, the final piece in the natural science exhibition was added: a human penis.

70 DON'T SLIP UP

The elf officer in Reykjavík is probably the only state employee in the world who looks after the well-being of trolls, elves, and other mysterious creatures. The official, who is well versed in mythology, knows where her (sometimes beastly) charges live and checks that planning applications are elf friendly. Tourists should not joke about it, since 50 percent of Icelanders believe in the *huldufolk*, the "hidden people."

N, BUT ......
HMAKER BAR.

KER ❤ BAR ❤

LISDOONVARNA
match-making
festival
❤
Meet
your
match!
Meet
Willie Daly
MATCHMAKER

"THE AIR IN...
...NVARNA" ❤ ❤
❤

This bar in Lisdoonvarna
hosts a matchmaking
festival, Irish style (no. 64).

71 NEW YEAR

Italy. The Italian custom, which is also popular in Spain, of wearing red underwear on New Year's Eve is said to guarantee love over the next twelve months. However, these special undergarments should be a present from your sweetheart. Consequently, red undies and boxer shorts of every fashion are on sale, both cheap versions and the pricey kind. The latter are exempt from the custom's commandment: "Destroy after New Year's!" Nevertheless, you can expect a new and beautiful red pair within a year.

72 A COWBOY IN TUSCANY

Maremma. Cowboys in Tuscany? Strange but true. In the once wild Maremma region, the mounted *butteri* herded cattle, which are sometimes still free roaming. They are predominantly hobby *butteri*, and some of them even take tourists with them on tour (over the Azienda Agricola di Alberese). Cisterna di Latina, the *buttero* epicenter, hosts the *merca*, the Tuscan rodeo, in May and October.

73 FORTUNE-TELLING SNAKES

Cocullo. For the "festival of the snake catchers" (*rito dei serpari*) on the first Sunday in May, thousands of people crowd into the small mountain village of Cocullo between Rome and Pescara. The week before, the locals catch hundreds of snakes, which are then hung around the statue of Saint Dominic for the procession. Believers think the behavior of the creatures will predict the future.

74 INTERESTING DECORATIONS

Taormina-Castelmola. Maybe it's best not to take grandma to the Bar Turrisi in Via Pio IX. She would certainly enjoy the wealth of antiques that decorate the café, but would she like the innumerable erect penises that can be seen here? They are purportedly for protection against evil eyes.

Must see: the procession with snakes in the mountain village of Cocullo, which is located close to Rome (no. 73).

75 DON'T SLIP UP

Do you get up before dawn to put a towel over the best lounge chairs at the beach or the pool? It's best to refrain from this annoying habit, because it is prohibited in bella Italia and can end up being expensive. In Liguria, a tourist is reported to have paid a thousand-euro fine as punishment.

76 WELL-TRAVELED STONES

Croatia. What do the Trogir cathedral and the White House have in common with the Diocletian's Palace and the Austrian parliament building in Vienna? They all were built from the marble-like Brač stone, a white limestone quarried in the region around Splitska and Skrip. In ancient times, the Romans discovered the beauty and impressive effect of the Croatian stone, which is still mined today.

77 MATTERS FOR THE HEART

Zagreb. In 2005, a pair of artists fell out of love—but before they split up, they established the Museum of Broken Relationships. The word spread, and people from around the world sent in the remainders of their broken relationships: a wedding dress, teddy bears, and so on. Although the museum was a success, it could not mend the couple's love.

78 NAKED TRUTHS ON RAB

Rab. When King Edward VIII of England and Lady Simpson skinny-dipped in the Mediterranean Sea off the coast of Rab in 1936, His Majesty inadvertently invented nudist tourism. Rab became the naturist epicenter, and as a result Croatia became a famous vacation destination. Edward's Kandarola Bay, which is still a nudist beach today, effectively became a monument to the "King's new clothes."

79 MALARIA-FREE ZONE FOR THE HEAD OF STATE

Brijuni. Without the help of Nobel Prize winner Robert Koch from Berlin, Yugoslavia's head of state Josip Broz Tito would have struggled to turn the once sealed-off island of Brijuni into his refuge. A previous owner had asked Koch to wipe out malaria on the island. The island of Vanga, which was once Tito's private property, is still closed to the public, but the main island of Veliki Brijun—with its exotic zoo—can be visited.

80 DON'T SLIP UP

Like their Slovenian neighbors, Croatia is a member of the European Union. However, unlike Slovenia, it is not part of the Eurozone, although the euro is used in everyday life, and prices for many goods are shown in euros. The Croatians see themselves as central European and not eastern European. Correspondingly, they are offended if you classify their country as eastern Europe or, even worse, as a Balkan state.

81 HOPPING REMEMBRANCE

Echternach. Word has spread about the "Echternach hopping procession," Luxembourg's most well-known religious event. The dance of "three steps forward, two steps back" is often used as a metaphor to criticize politicians. However, on Whit Tuesday (the day after Pentecost Monday), the residents of Echternach do not actually hop backward and forward (anymore), but from right to left and always just a little forward. It is all in memory of Saint Willibrord, the apostle of the Frisians.

82 THE LAST OF ITS KIND

Luxembourg. The Grand Duchy of Luxembourg is the only monarchy in the world that bears this title. There were once about a dozen grand duchies, including the Grand Duchy of Frankfurt. After the Congress of Vienna, there were only eight. The title goes back to the pope, who honored Tuscany with it in 1569. Napoleon adopted the idea and created further grand duchies in Germany and Luxembourg.

83 THE MOSELLE AGREEMENT

Schengen. The Schengen Agreement, which paved the way for free movement in Europe, was not signed in Schengen, Luxembourg, but close by on the ship *Princesse Marie-Astrid* on the Moselle tri-border in 1985. It was the second boat christened in honor of the princess and later sailed on the Danube under the name MS *Regensburg*.

84 MULTILINGUAL INFORMATION

Luxembourg. *Luxemburger Wort* is the only newspaper in the world to carry articles in three languages, and it is published in the grand duchy. The majority of the articles are written in German, with approximately 16 percent in French and 2 percent in Luxembourgian, the dialect that has developed over centuries in this region. In addition, the online edition of the *Wort* offers stories in Portuguese, because more than 10 percent of the population originates from Portugal.

85 DON'T SLIP UP ————— —————

Please don't make any jokes about the size of Luxembourg. No, not because the inhabitants are too sensitive—they are simply bored because they already know all Luxembourg jokes . . . absolutely all of them. An example: "What would the German army do if Luxembourg invaded Germany? Nothing—they will let the fire department in Trier sort it out." And another tip for Luxembourgian etiquette: always eat cake with a knife and fork.

86 BAN ON ROWDY PARTIES

Malta. In the really devout island state, each village celebrates its patron saint on their name day with a large *festa*. At least most of them do, but the local priests are entitled to put a stop to the celebrations if they feel that the congregation will celebrate without due reverence and may become too exuberant (meaning too much drink and less-than-modest dancing).

87 GOOD EATERS

Malta. Those with a tendency for corpulence will be in good company if they vacation on the Mediterranean island of Malta. According to a study by the European Union, the Maltese are statistically the plumpest citizens in the EU. Their average body mass index is 26.6, while the rest of the EU has a BMI of 25.4. (Anything over 25 is considered "overweight.")

88 THE FLAG WITH THE CROSS

Malta. The island's flag is decorated with the Saint George's Cross, which is also the second-highest military order awarded by Great Britain. Malta is the only country to receive this honor, because during World War II, the Maltese bravely endured constant bombardment. However, the cross cannot be used as a merchant flag, because it looks similar to a maritime signal flag that means "pilot on board." Instead, Maltese ships fly the Maltese cross with pointed ends.

89 CHIVALROUS WINE

Cyprus. The oldest sweet wine in the world is the Cypriot *commandaria*. It is said to have been first pressed in 2000 BCE. However, its current name is somewhat younger. At the end of the thirteenth century, when the knights of the Order of Saint John established the Grande Commanderie, their base on Cyprus, they gave this specialty its name. It has now become an international brand name.

90 DON'T SLIP UP

There is a legend that Cypriots very much dislike and is best not to mention. When God was handing out gifts to the nations, the Cypriots came too late. Everything had already been distributed. But the islanders insisted on receiving a present. And so the Lord handed the Cypriots something that was left over because nobody wanted it: intrigue.

91 COUNTRY OF OPPRESSORS

Moldova / Ukraine. Bessarabia—isn't that one of the Arab emirates? No, Bessarabia is actually one of the most frequent geographical mistakes. The term is used to denote the territory on which the modern-day eastern European countries of Moldova and Ukraine stand. The old name goes back to the fourteenth century and the *Bessarab* ("oppressors") dynasty. No wonder Moldova picked a new name for itself!

92 THE BIGGEST WINE CELLAR IN THE WORLD

Moldova. The country holds one world record that—at least at first glance—is invisible: the biggest wine cellar in the world. If you want to take a tour, be sure to bring along a picnic (drinks are provided), because the network of tunnels measures approximately 78 miles (125 kilometers). Furthermore, the small country also keeps the largest collection of wines down there: two million bottles, including vintages from Hermann Göring's estate.

93 MEN PARTYING IN WOMEN'S CLOTHES

Ukraine. The evening of January 13 is the Ukrainian celebration of Saint Melania. The festivities can get a little wild, particularly in the villages. Men dress up as ugly women and go from house to house in groups, causing all kinds of mischief. Once upon a time, this charade was a ruse for the young, masked men to secretly meet unmarried daughters.

94 VERY DEEP UNDERGROUND

Kyiv. The Kyiv Metro's Arsenalna station is located 344 feet (105 meters) below the surface and is therefore the deepest underground station in the world. It was built in 1960, and rumors circulate in the Ukrainian capital that it is also a bunker for politicians and that is why it is so deep. Incidentally, the Ukrainian parliament is located near the station.

95 DON'T SLIP UP

According to the World Health Organization, Moldova and Ukraine are two of the five countries with the highest alcohol consumption. This is something that visitors also experience, usually by receiving an invitation for a glass of vodka. If you say no, you are regarded with suspicion. However, medical reasons are an acceptable excuse; for example, it is considered a good reason to abstain if you have just taken some pills. Incidentally, the other three countries in the top five are Russia, Hungary, and the Czech Republic.

96 LIVING LIKE A KING

Monaco. With approximately thirty-two thousand inhabitants living in just over 1.24 square miles (2 square kilometers), Monaco wins the title of the most densely populated country in the world. At the same time, it also has the most expensive average real estate prices. Nevertheless, properties in the income-tax-free microstate are very sought after.

97 LOOK BUT DON'T PLAY

Monaco. The inhabitants of Monaco, just like citizens of some other areas with casinos, may not set foot in their palaces of fortune. Roulette and the like should remain discretely separated from daily life. Therefore, the croupiers never refer to each other in public by name. However, it is no longer true that the casinos financially prop up the principality. Gambling now contributes only 5 percent to the state's budget.

98 ROCKIN' THE ROULETTE

Monaco. Mick Jagger would be wise to refrain from visiting the Casino Monte Carlo. A distant relative of his, Joseph Jagger, was the first gambler to clear out the fledgling casino. In 1875, he noticed that a roulette wheel wobbled and therefore some numbers came up more often. As a result, he won 60,000 pounds sterling in three days. In today's money, that would be 3,000,000 pounds sterling—or nearly $4 million!

99 WHERE NOBLE VINTAGES ARE STORED

Monaco. The cellar keepers of the legendary Hôtel de Paris must have good walking boots. In order to fetch a bottle from the backmost shelf, they have to walk 1.24 miles (2 kilometers) in the world's biggest single-owner wine cellar. The 16,146-square-foot (1,500 square meter) vaulted cave under the hotel holds around 350,000 of the most noble wines.

100 DON'T SLIP UP

Real Monacans are a minority in Monaco. You are most likely to meet them in the Old Town in the evening. They are proud of their small feudal state and hold the Grimaldis in great esteem. However, what they do not like is the gossip that is spread about their (not necessarily always) noble heads by certain tabloids in Germany and Great Britain, which rarely has a grain of truth to it. Definitely not a good topic for small talk.

101 BITTERS AND (ORANGE) ROOT VEGETABLES

The Netherlands. Koningsdag on April 27 is a public holiday and the birthday of King Willem-Alexander of the Netherlands. To celebrate, the whole country wears orange—the color of the House of Orange—and the people drink Oranje bitter, an orange spirit. Only the carrots are not given due appreciation, yet they have an interesting orange history. The vegetable was either red or white until the seventeenth century, when it was cultivated in orange in honor of William of Orange.

102 DRY RUN FOR BATHING SEASON

Amsterdam. Even though it is usually still a bit chilly at the start of May, young people clad in swimwear, snorkels, diving masks, and flippers meet for the national flipper race on the Dam Square in the heart of the city. One participant told a gullible journalist that the event was to highlight seawater floods. However, it has one primary purpose: to have a great party.

103 LONDON IN THE NETHERLANDS

Deventer. For one weekend in Advent, the area around Walstraat in this small town becomes Victorian London for the Charles Dickens Festival. A regally waving Queen Victoria is carried through the streets in a sedan chair. Ebenezer Scrooge, Oliver Twist, and David Copperfield also make an appearance, and around one thousand performers wear Dickensian costumes.

104 COUPLES ON THEIR OWN

Vlieland. Engaged couples have discovered the "loneliest place in the Netherlands" for marriage ceremonies. It is a small rescue hut for shipwrecks or those in danger of floods on the Vlieland sandbank in the mudflats. The Drenkelingenhuisje, which stands on eight stilts, is actually a beachcombers' museum and has been an outpost of the East Vlieland register office since 1997.

105 DON'T SLIP UP

"Everyone in Holland speaks German." This statement, which is frequently repeated in Germany, contains two mistakes. The inhabitants of the Netherlands do not like it when we use the word "Holland" to describe "the Netherlands" as the same thing, because only two of the twelve provinces in the country form part of Holland. And not everybody can or wants to speak German, at least not when it is expected that they answer in German. It is better to ask, preferably in English, which language is better.

106 GLOBETROTTING RATS WITH A PSEUDONYM

Norway. "Norway rats," which are now found almost everywhere in the world, are not originally from Norway but northern China. It is from there that these traveling rats reached western Europe. In the sixteenth century, the rats are said to have stowed away on a Norwegian ship bound for Britain—and then two hundred years later, they sailed from England to America.

Koningsdag on April 27 is a public holiday in the Netherlands, and the whole country wears orange, the color of the House of Orange, to celebrate (no. 101).

107 YOU CAN ALWAYS GO FARTHER NORTH

North Cape. Every year, thousands of tourists visit the North Cape to experience the "northernmost point on mainland Europe," which lies approximately 1,305 miles (2,100 kilometers) from the North Pole. Unfortunately, they are in the wrong place. The cliff is on an island, and the real northernmost point of mainland Europe is next door on the Knivskjellodden peninsula.

108 DEEP FREEZE FOR SEEDS

Spitsbergen. At Longyearbyen, there is a concrete archway with steel doors in the bluff that leads to the "global seed vault." Deep in the permafrost, 2.25 billion seeds of important crops such as rice, corn, and potatoes are stored in an earthquake-proof and nuclear-bomb-proof vault. In the event of catastrophes or genetic losses, the seeds are intended to ensure the survival of humanity. The tunnels are maintained via automation from Sweden.

109 THE SMALLEST HOTEL IN THE WORLD

Spitsbergen. Just a few cruise passengers are acquainted with the Lloyd's Hotel: a shelter built in 1905 by the sailors from a cruise ship owned by North German Lloyd. The little hut decorated with souvenirs is still used for land excursions from Hapag-Lloyd vessels. As part of the ritual, the crew serves mulled wine and Lumumba (a beverage involving cocoa and rum) in the "smallest hotel in the world."

110 DON'T SLIP UP

In the Nordic countries, the word for "thank you" is *takk*. However, in Norwegian you should never use the phrase *takk for alt* ("thank you for everything"). It is traditionally reserved for eulogies, funeral wreaths, and gravestones. Furthermore, Norwegians don't like it when they are generally spoken of as Scandinavian, and they share this reservation with the Danes, Swedes, Finns, and Icelanders, despite good Nordic neighborly relations.

111 DELICIOUS FALL

Austria. There is a great to-do about the Goldene Sennerharfe prize, which has been running for more than twenty-five years. At the end of September, a good hundred Alpine herdsmen come down from their meadows to Galtür in Tyrol to participate. They bring with them the best cheese they produced over the summer in the mountains. It is entered into the Alps cheese championship, and the cheese is judged by a jury of specialists. Will the honor go to Germany, Italy, Liechtenstein, or Switzerland, or will it stay in Austria? And to whom will the children's jury give their prize? And, last but not least, the public can also taste the cheeses.

112 EAT LIKE MOZART'S CONTEMPORARIES

Salzburg. Where better than in Mozart's Austrian hometown to enjoy an eighteenth-century meal? The St. Peter Stiftskulinarium, which was established more than twelve hundred years ago, invites diners to the Mozart Dinner, served in the baroque room of the monastery. It is composed of roast capon with red wine and herb glacé, as well as potato gratin—and a side of background music played by musicians in correct period costume, naturally.

113 STANDING OVATIONS RECORD

Vienna. An evening at the Vienna State Opera is the highpoint of many trips to the capital of Austria. But it can be a rather long affair. The theater has the record for the most number of curtain calls: the applause lasted one hour and twenty minutes for Placido Domingo's performance of Verdi's opera *Otello* in 1991. The famous tenor had to return to the stage 101 times after his rendering of the drama of jealousy.

114 FAKE UPON FAKE

Vienna. For as long as there have been successful artists, there have been forgeries of their work. However, a new development is forgeries of forgeries. Some have even made it into the museum—the Vienna Museum of Art Fakes, that is. In this museum, what is written on the label is at least true. Experts believe that one in ten pictures held in museums around the world are fake.

115 DON'T SLIP UP

It is well known in Germany that Austrians like to call their German neighbors *Piefke*, meaning pompous and German—and it is not exactly meant affectionately. Maybe they have a reason for it, because the Germans often like to annoy them with the fact that Hitler was born in Austria, not Germany. Or because Germans sometimes try to imitate the Austrian dialect, horribly twisting the language in the process.

116 WATER, WATER EVERYWHERE

Poland. For Polish women—especially young and pretty ones—and also for female tourists, Easter Monday can be a dangerous day. Throughout the country and particularly in the countryside, water—be it in water pistols or buckets—awaits them. Men, mainly of the young variety, will try to soak the women and girls. Previously a courtship ritual, "wet Monday" is traced back to King Mieszko I, who was the first ruler to be baptized.

117 A CITY OWNED BY DWARFS

Wrocław. Small bronze dwarfs with pointed hats doing all kinds of jobs are found all over the city. There are said to be more than two hundred statues, and finding them all is almost impossible. The diminutive 12-inch-high (30 centimeter) figures are the legacy of the Polish uprising against the former Communist regime. The Wrocław artists thought them up as a creative protest.

118 A SALTY MUSICAL TREAT

Kraków. A church—including the altar and the pulpit—made entirely of salt is the underground attraction in the Wieliczka salt mine, close to Kraków. In 1697, miners created the house of God, which is 177 feet (54 meters) long (177 ft), 59 feet (18 meters) wide, and 39 feet (12 meters) high—and 331 feet (101 meters) underground, with an air humidity of 70 percent. Today, thanks to its good acoustics, it is also used for concerts. The audience generally wears thick sweaters because the constant temperature is 57°F (14°C).

119 THE CROOKED PINE FOREST

Gryfino. Close to the German border grows a unique forest, the "crooked forest." Although its pines sprout directly up from the ground, after about one month they turn on their sides until the trunks rest on the ground. From then on, they continue to grow straight up again. It is thought that this mysterious growth of the trees is due to a method previously used by lumberjacks.

120 DON'T SLIP UP

Poland is one of the most Roman Catholic countries in Europe, but still superstition is rife here. Hence, never offer your hand to your host over the threshold of their home, because it brings bad luck. You never put your handbag on the floor, because "the money runs away." Incidentally, a different kind of superstition would be to believe that Poland's drivers would stop for pedestrians at crosswalks.

121 BIOLOGICAL PEST CONTROL

Coimbra. Cats and bats help protect old valuable books in the Baroque Library at the University of Coimbra in Portugal. At some point, bats started roosting in the library, which was inaugurated in 1728. The bats eat insects during the night, and each evening leather mats are laid over mahogany tables—which are at least as valuable as the books—in order to protect them from bat droppings. Furthermore, under the fly zone, the cats keep watch for rats and mice.

122 THE FLINTSTONES' HOME

Fafe. Cartoon hero Fred Flintstone and his Stone Age family were the inspiration behind the Casa do Penedo, located close to Fafe in northern Portugal. The much-photographed "stone house" is located between two large boulders. *Forbes* magazine counted the house among "the best hidden homes in the world." It is privately owned and can be viewed only from the outside.

123 DOWN TO THE BONE

Èvora. This city, one of the most beautiful historic cities in Portugal, is the home not only to the Roman Temple of Diana and a cathedral, but also to the Capela dos Ossos ("Chapel of Bones"). The walls of the special little church are embedded with human bones and skulls. An inscription reminds visitors that one day, they too will be only bones.

124 ORNITHOLOGICAL MISTAKE

Azores. The Azores owe their name to a mistake regarding natural history. When Portuguese explorers landed on the islands, they noticed there were a lot of hawks there. So they called the archipelago Ilhas dos Açores ("Islands of Hawks"). Later, upon the arrival of Portuguese with better knowledge of feathered fauna, it was determined that these hawks were actually buzzards. However, the name stayed.

125 DON'T SLIP UP ——————— ———

Attention, shorts wearers! Portuguese people of both sexes think it is ridiculous for men to wear shorts when not on the beach. In churches or public buildings, they are even considered offensive. And the Portuguese also deem it very impolite if foreigners want to talk to them about Spain. Even Spanish football is not a good topic, since the majority of the folks from Portugal have nothing good to say about that either.

126 HERBS AGAINST TAX

Romania. Certainly, the Danube is not as blue as the waltz suggests. But is it poisoned? It really did happen in Romania, and the poison used was mandrake, a plant from the nightshade family. For witches, this hallucinogenic plant is indispensable. In 2011, Romanian witches used it to curse the Romanian president and government because they suddenly demanded taxes of 16 percent from the ladies. As if curses would influence politicians . . .

127 THE EXPERT WHO NEVER SET FOOT IN TRANSYLVANIA

Transylvania. The Irish author Bram Stoker made Romania, or at least Transylvania, famous with his book *Dracula*. Many fans search for traces of his blood-hungry count, normally with a travel guide in hand. However, the author did not go to the bother of visiting himself; in his whole life, he was never in Transylvania. He took his local knowledge from the *Austria-Hungary Baedeker*, the travel guide of his time.

128 LIES ABOUT THE BRIDGE OF LIES

Sibiu. The legend that the "Bridge of Lies" in Sibiu immediately punishes lies—for example, by throwing to the floor brides who are dishonest about their virginity—is a lie itself. The beautiful cast-iron construction, made in Hesse, Germany, was originally called the lying bridge quite simply because it lies in place at each end without any support in between.

129 THE HAPPY CEMETERY

Săpânța. The majority of the wooden tombstones in the graveyard in Săpânța were created by a local artist using colorful and happy images, reliefs, and sayings as per the motto "Only speak good of the dead." But this "Happy Cemetery" is worth a second, more critical glance: on the reverse of some crosses, the little weaknesses of the deceased have also been illustrated.

130 SUMMER SOLSTICE

St. Petersburg. North of the Arctic Circle, the sun doesn't set on the summer solstice. The star only briefly dips below the horizon, but it still illuminates the sky for the famous "white nights." During that time, St. Petersburg is magical. In the northernmost metropolis, the celebrations last all night, reaching a high point when the scarlet-sailed brigantine comes down the Neva River. It is in honor of the year's new school graduates, all of whom have surely read Fyodor Dostoevsky's "White Nights."

131 STRAIGHT, BUT WITH A CURVE

Moscow / St. Petersburg. The "Czar's finger," a meander on the otherwise straight railroad between Moscow and St. Petersburg, is said to have come about because when drawing the connection between the cities with a ruler, the monarch also outlined the tip of his finger. However, the truth is the train had to avoid a steep gradient there. But now the legend is history: in 2001, the stretch was straightened.

132 A BISHOP IN THE SAUNA

St. Petersburg. The Lutheran Church of Saint Peter and Saint Paul, the denomination's biggest in Russia, was converted into an 82-foot-long (25 meter) swimming pool during Soviet times. Today, prayers are once again said atop the pool covering (removing the basin would cause the church to collapse), and the bishop's office is located in a former sauna.

133 BEAUTIFUL RED SQUARE

Moscow. Red Square in Moscow is not the powerful monument of the Communist era that the name may suggest. Krasnaya ploshchad', as the world-famous square is known in Russian, means "beautiful square," and that was already its name in the sixteenth century. The other possible linguistic meaning, "red square," was naturally more appealing to the men behind the red walls of the Kremlin.

134 CATHERINE AND HER LOVERS

Pushkin. The tour guides of the majestic Catherine Palace in Pushkin constantly have to answer questions about the empress's "sex addiction." Is it true that her personal physician examined her lovers? Probably yes, for fear of diseases. Is it true that her ladies-in-waiting were used as guinea pigs before Catherine? Most likely not. Was the empress insatiable? Hmm, well, there were fewer than twenty lovers.

135 SUMMER SOLSTICE

Sweden. For the Swedes, *midsommar* is a huge celebration between June 20 and 26. However, the name meaning "midsummer" is incorrect, because officially summer is just starting and does not end until September 22 or 23. And the festival's symbol: the *majstång*—a May pole in late June? The decorated pole's name comes from the word *maja*, meaning decorated with flowers. Speaking of flowers, young girls collect seven types of flowers in the night. If they place them under their pillow, they will dream of their future husband.

136 NO BOARDING FOR ROTTEN FOOD

Sweden. The delicacy *surströmming* is certainly an acquired taste. It is herring that has fermented in brine for at least three months (and then stinks to high heaven) before it is packed in tins. Since it continues to ferment in the can, there is a risk of explosion. Therefore, taking it on board Air France and British Airways flights has been prohibited.

137 EATING LIKE A NOBEL PRIZE WINNER

Stockholm. After the award ceremony for the Nobel Prize each year on December 10 in Stockholm, the 1,300 guests are served a celebratory banquet at the *stadshuskällaren* ("town hall cellar"). Mere mortals can also enjoy the dinner after prior registration. Historical menus can be arranged for groups of eight or more, so visitors can eat the same food as their favorite award recipients.

138 ENTICING PLACE NAME

Fjuckby. The small town of Fjuckby ("windy place"), located close to Uppsala, will continue to live with its name—and with some ridicule. A few years ago, some residents requested a new name because the old one was associated with "certain pleasures of the flesh" both in Swedish (*juck*) and in English (f**k). The authorities rejected the application because it was not supported by enough Fjuckbyers.

139 PROTOTYPES ON ICE

Arjeplog. The northern Swedish village is unknown to most people in the world, unless they work in the car-manufacturing industry. There, more or less disguised prototypes are tested on the frozen lake of the automobile industry's "winter center." Consequently, more and more paparazzi lurk nearby, and the village's only gas station is "the most photographed" in the world.

140 DON'T SLIP UP

In Sweden, you are more likely to slip on margarine or butter than a banana. Each spread has its own special knife (just like the cheese and ham, etc.), which is placed back on the plate of food once used. In addition, everyone is addressed using the informal *du* (but not necessarily always with the first name).

141 THE SCIENCE OF HOLES

Switzerland. Cheese is becoming less holey. The observation is strange but true, and it's a serious problem for the Swiss. Better filters in the dairy components mean that the cheese lacks hay dust, so there are fewer holes. Organic "dust" is now added to the cheese so that Emmental and the likes still keep their traditional appearance. And how do the cheese experts check whether the blocks are developing good holes? With the modern medical technology—namely, a CT scan.

142 THE COW QUEEN

Martigny. Every October, an audience of fifty thousand people crams into Martigny stadium to watch the final of the Swiss cow contest and see who will be crowned "queen of queens." The bovine ladies do not need a toreador; they simply try to assert their dominance as the mistress of the ring, without drawing blood from their competitors. The winner receives a new bell.

143 UNDERCOVER UNDER THE MOUNTAINS

Vitznau. The Swiss mountains are said to be as holey as their cheese, since there are bunkers and military tunnels everywhere. However, the military compounds are no longer needed. Vitznau, located close to Lucerne, has converted one into a bunker hotel, complete with military equipment and army ambiance. It allows groups to become cheaply acquainted with the former state defenses below the ground. Army sleeping bags and wool blankets embellished with the Swiss cross are available at an extra charge.

144 THE LONGEST STAIRS IN THE WORLD

Niesen, close to Wimmis. The longest stairs in the world are accessible to the public only once a year. Interested climbers must first register on time for the Lauf auf den Niesen ("Run up the Niesen"). The race goes up the 11,674 service stairs along the funicular track. It covers 2.11 miles (3.4 kilometers), starting at an altitude of 2,296 feet (700 meters) and rising up to 7,753 feet (2,363 meters), and has an average incline of 55 percent. The record finish time is around one hour.

145 DELICIOUS FALL

Vevey. Wine festivals take place all over Europe, but the Fête des Vignerons in Vevey is unique. It happens only every twenty-five years, and then six thousand people (almost one in three inhabitants) play a part. The crowd scenes in historic costumes are a high point of the show. The audience comes from the whole world. The last *fête* was held from mid-July to mid-August in 2019. UNESCO has awarded it status for "intangible cultural heritage."

146 TRIO OF CAPITALS

Bratislava. Slovakia's capital is the only capital in the world whose municipal area borders on two other countries: Austria and Hungary. Bratislava, which until 1919 was also officially known as Pressburg, is connected via the Danube to the capitals of Austria (Vienna) and Hungary (Budapest). The journey time from Bratislava to Vienna by catamaran is just seventy-five minutes. The water jet's motor allows the vessel to reach speeds of approximately 37 miles per hour (60 kilometers per hour).

147 A WINE FOR THE SAINTS

Prague. On November 11, the capital of the Czech Republic celebrates Saint Martin's Day with an old custom: the vintners market next to the city hall serves the first Martin's wine of the year. This wine traditionally comes from five different vines: three types of grapes for white wine and two for red wine. Saint Martin on his horse tastes the new vintage personally.

148 HORSES HANGING FROM THE CEILING

Prague. The Lucerna in Prague is considered to be one of the most beautiful movie theaters in Europe. Underneath a glass dome in its large foyer hangs a bizarre artifact: a statue of Saint Wenceslas on a mount. However, he is sitting on the dead horse's stomach and not its back, as a parody of the equestrian statue in Prague's Wenceslas Square.

149 CITY OF VAMPIRES

Český Krumlov. The existence of vampires in Český Krumlov has been "proven" by the presence of three-hundred-year-old skeletons, which were buried and weighed down with stones. To boot, one of them had been beheaded, and another has a stake where its heart would have been. The town was also the home of noblewoman Eleonore von Schwarzenberg, who is famed for drinking wolf's milk in order to conceive a son. In reality, she was suffering from cancer and is buried in the church of Saint Vitus; her heart was separately immured.

150 DON'T SLIP UP

The Czechs love academic titles, and those who have gained them want to be addressed with them. And those who haven't? They won't contradict you if you politely address them as "master engineer" or "doctor" or even "professor" if you suspect higher intelligence. And what is a good conversation starter with the Czechs? Ice hockey is always a good topic.

151 THE OLDEST GRAPEVINE IN THE WORLD

Maribor. In Slovenia's second biggest city, the world's oldest living grapevine has been growing for around four hundred years. Every year, it still produces enough grapes to make 20 liters of žametovka wine. It is decanted into one hundred beautiful quarter-liter bottles, which are popular thanks to their rarity and not necessarily on account of the quality of the wine.

152 POLITICS UNDER THE LINDEN

Ludranski Vrh. The national symbol of Slovenia, the Najevnik linden tree in Ludranski Vrh, is 79 feet (24 meters) high and has a trunk circumference of 35 feet (10.7 meters). The linden tree has lived through important moments of Slovenian history, such as the Ottoman invasion. It dates back to the era of the legendary King Matjaž. It is now a tradition for Slovenia's political elite to meet under its crown each summer.

153 BRIDGE BUILDING

Jesenice / Nova Gorica. The Solkan Bridge on the line between Jesenice and Nova Gorica is the largest stone railway bridge in the world. Believe it or not, its main arch was constructed in 1927 by using 4,533 rocks cut to fit exactly. The arch alone is 118 feet (36 meters) high and 279 feet (85 meters) long. In total, the Solkan Bridge measures just under 722 feet (220 meters). The railroad was built on behalf of the imperial and royal government in Vienna.

154 NOT JUST OVER THE THRESHOLD, BUT UP THE STAIRS

Bled. "Slovenia's only island" is in Lake Bled. The Church of the Assumption of Mary on the island was built in 1465 and holds several art treasures. Brides from Slovenia and farther afield like to choose this church for their wedding ceremonies. But does the groom know that according to the tradition, he is supposed to carry his bride up the ninety-nine steps of the outside staircase?

155 DON'T SLIP UP ——— ———

If you are invited to the home of a Slovenian, you must expect to be offered a *slivovitz* (plum spirit) or *boroviča* (juniper spirit), even during the day. It is usually a strong distillate and, especially in rural areas, expected to be of the home-brewed variety. Be careful: as soon as you empty your glass, it will be refilled. If you don't want more, then you should always visibly leave some of the drink in the glass as a polite signal.

156 NEW YEAR

Spain. The epicenter of Spanish New Year's Eve celebrations is Madrid City Hall. When the tower clock strikes twelve, the majority of the nation swallows one grape per strike, each symbolizing a month of the new year. But this is easier said than done. Due to reports of choking, the time between the strikes has been increased from one to three seconds. The custom was begun by Spanish vintners, who wanted to dispose of some of their abundant harvest in 1909.

157 WHEN THE DEVIL JUMPS OVER BABIES

Castrillo de Murcia. The Salto del Colacho ("devil's jump") is one of the strangest customs in custom-rich Spain. Every year on the Saturday after the feast of Corpus Christi, devils dressed in yellow and red have insults hurled at them, primarily by children. The so-called *colachos* defend themselves with bullwhips. On Sunday, they jump over babies to release them from their sins and protect them against all evil.

No. 157 explains why devils jump over babies in Castrillo de Murcia in Spain.

158 BLUE HOUSES IN THE WHITE VILLAGE

Júzcar. This village is one of the famous "white villages" of Andalusia, despite all the houses having been painted blue. They were turned blue as part of the advertisement for the Spanish premiere of a Smurf film. After the end of the campaign, the majority of the inhabitants asked for the bright blue to be kept because it was attracting more visitors to the village.

159 THE INCOMPLETE RECYCLED CATHEDRAL

Mejorada del Campo. One of the most unusual cathedrals in the world, located in Mejorada del Campo, is the work of farmer Justo Gallego Martinez, who—after recovering from an illness—promised to construct a large church with his own hands despite not having any knowledge of architecture. Since he did not have much money, he and his two helpers worked on building the recycled church with any materials they could find or were given since 1961. Gallego passed away at age ninety-six in his cathedral in November 2021.

160 DON'T SLIP UP

Eating is a big thing in Spain; an hour for lunch is considered rather short. Incidentally *paella* is eaten only at lunchtime. If you order the dish in the evening, you out yourself as a tourist before even taking the first bite. In the evening, there is a wonderful alternative: *tapas* as part of a pub crawl. Make sure you always ask for the house specialty.

161 SWIM FROM ONE CONTINENT TO ANOTHER

Istanbul. The largest city in Turkey is the only city in the world located on two continents. The European part in the northwest is separated from the Asian part in the southeast by the Bosporus Strait. Each July, Istanbul hosts the unique Cross Continental Swim in the strait, which is only 2,297 to 7,546 feet (700 to 2,300 meters) wide. For two hours, ships have no access to the Bosporus, and the swimmers rule the waves.

162 FLUFFY CAPITAL

Ankara. Until 1930, the name of the Turkish capital, Ankara, was actually Angora. It was either derived from the rabbits of the region with their distinctive fluffy coat or from the angora goat, which gave mohair to fashion. Angora rabbits were the first bunnies that became pets. After the French royal family discovered them, the rest of France's elite wanted the "Turkish bunnies."

163 THRIFTY BUILDER

Istanbul. The Sultan Ahmed Mosque in Istanbul, better known as the "Blue Mosque," is one of the few Islamic places of worship with six minarets (towers). Sultan Ahmed I had commissioned the architect to plate the four planned minarets with gold. However, the required amount of sheet gold would have blown the budget out of the water. And, so, the builder "misheard" *altin* ("gold") and built *alti* ("six") minarets instead.

164 WRESTLING CAMELS

Selçuk. On the west coast of Turkey, "camel wrestling" season starts in the winter. The timing enables owners to take advantage of the normally calm animals' instinct to dominate during the mating season from November to March. When wrestling, two camels try to push each other down—generally a short "fight." Many festivals have sprung up from the erstwhile nomad entertainment. Selçuk is the center of the professional league.

165 DON'T SLIP UP

The founding father of modern Turkey, Kemal Atatürk, appears on Turkish paper money. Writing on the counterfeit-proof front or back of the bill is considered an insult to the statesman, who is still held in high regard today. So any "criminal" who writes on the money should expect punishment. Also, everyone is insulted when tourists haggle at the bazaar or the souvenir shop without any intention of buying. You also shouldn't haggle for small items.

166 MIND GAMES IN A WARM BATH

Budapest. Chess players meet daily in the outdoor thermal pools at Szechenyi Baths, Europe's biggest medicinal bath. The dandelion yellow baroque pool, whose water reaches temperatures of up to 165°F (74°C) and comes from almost 328 feet (1,000 meters) below the surface, is just one of around 1,500 thermal and hot springs in Europe.

167 DIVING UNDER THE CITY

Budapest. The Molnár lies under the Hungarian capital. It is a largely flooded system of caves, in which novice divers may not swim any deeper than 164 feet (50 meters) from the entrance. Even experienced divers do not explore the labyrinth of narrow tunnels and cathedral-like halls without a guide. Fossils of marine life have been found in the caves.

168 HONORING A NATIVE SON

Budapest / Raiding. Budapest International Airport is called Ferenc Liszt Airport. Franz Liszt's place of birth, Raiding, which is located in Burgenland in modern Austria, was Hungarian at the time of his birth. The composer did not speak Hungarian, just German and French. And he died in Bayreuth, Germany. However, Liszt described himself as Hungarian and also signed his name as "Liszt, Ferencz."

Combining two sports: chess in the swimming pool (no. 166).

169 A MECCA IN HUNGARY

Budapest. Gül Baba, a Muslim dervish and poet from the sixteenth century, arrived in Hungary with the Ottoman invasion and died there in 1541. His mausoleum in Mecset Street was used as a Catholic church after the Habsburgs reconquered Hungary. The small building, which is today owned by Turkey, is the northernmost shrine and place of pilgrimage in Islam.

170 DON'T SLIP UP

The Hungarians like a drink, but for many, particularly the older Magyars, beer has been a no-go since the 1848–49 revolution. The occupiers won, executed Hungarian generals, and celebrated with beer. As a result, the Hungarians decided not to raise beer tankards for 150 years. The vow ended in 1999, but it is still kept in some places.

171 SINNERS IN THE HOLIEST PLACE

Vatican City. It is common knowledge that the Vatican is the smallest state in the world. What is less known is that it is also the country with the highest rate of criminality. The Vatican has approximately seven hundred citizens and almost 1.2 million visitors each year, which attracts pickpockets. The offenses are normally just petty crime, but there was once a double murder.

172 IN SPITE OF THE DOUBTERS

Vatican City. The most famous statue in Saint Peter's Basilica is without question *Pietà* by Michelangelo. If you look closely, you will see the signature of the artist, who normally refrained from signing his other sculptures. However, Michelangelo is said to have heard two men of the cloth say that he was too young to have created this masterpiece. Legend has it that he then secretly sneaked into the church and signed the Mother of God.

173 STROKING THE GOLDEN FOOT

Vatican City. Another famous statue in Saint Peter's Basilica is the bronze statue of Saint Peter, whose right foot slightly protrudes. This foot has been well and truly rubbed, because it is supposed to bring a blessing if you touch it. Over the course of the centuries, the foot is said to have been replaced several times. The monument was created around 1300 by Arnolfo di Cambio. On high holidays, the sculpture is clad in bishop's robes.

174 A BETTER VIEW OF HEAVEN

Castel Gandolfo. The grounds of the papal summer residence also host the Vatican's observatory. It had to leave Rome due to the high level of "light pollution." But even here, at 1,398 feet (426 meters) above sea level in the Alban Hills, the view of higher bodies is generally impeded. Therefore, in 1993, the Vatican stationed another telescope on Mount Graham in southwestern Arizona.

175 DON'T SLIP UP

Any ordinary Christian will wait in vain for a private audience with Pontifex Maximus. At best, they may be granted a group audience. However, on Wednesdays at 10:30 a.m., if they follow the protocol of covering shoulders and knees and not carrying knives, other metal objects, or glass bottles, they have a good chance of a general audience along with ten thousand others. After a short speech by the pope and a prayer, they can leave having been blessed.

176 THE HEALING POWER OF BIRCHES

Belarus. Of course, the Belarusians enjoy vodka, like the residents of nearly all the nations in eastern Europe. But they also have another fluid favorite that they generally drink unfermented: birch juice. In spring, the liquid is tapped from the trees. At this time of year, a healthy birch provides up to 10 liters of juice per day. The natural product is said to have a healing effect against gout and rheumatism, although this has not been medically proven.

177 A HERO OF THE WHOLE WORLD

Mieračoŭščyna. Tadeusz Kościuszko is a national hero not only in Poland and the US (where he fought alongside George Washington), but also in Belarus. The Polish noble was born in 1746 in **Mieračoŭščyna**, a town that is today part of Belarus. All around the world, Polish expatriates build monuments for Kościuszko, and even the highest mountain in Australia was named for him.

178 PAPAL LOVE OF BUFFALO

Belovezhskaya Pushcha. Belarus has the biggest herd of bison in the world. The animals live mainly in Belovezhskaya Pushcha, the world's biggest virgin forest, which was already placed under protection in the fourteenth century. The Belarusians are proud of their bison, whose fans appear to reach all the way to Rome. Pope Leo X is reported to have once asked poet Mikola Gusovski to write a bison poem.

179 PURELY MEN'S BUSINESS

Slutsk. The majority of the original Slutsk belts, once worn by the Belarusian nobility, have disappeared from collections around the world. Even Belarus itself owns only a couple of the sashes, which are up to approximately 13 feet (4 meters) long and often have gold and silver threads woven into them. In the past, only men were allowed to weave and wear them. Recently, production has begun again, and they are sold as souvenirs for tourists.

180 DON'T SLIP UP

In the West, Belarus is thought of as the "last dictatorship in Europe," which is likely one of the reasons for the low number of visitors to the country. Tourists should be careful not to mention this dubious honor and avoid talking about President Alexander Lukashenko, politics in general, or the country's economic situation. Such talk could be punished with expulsion or worse sanctions.

On Maho Beach on the island of Saint Martin, airplanes thunder by, just feet over swimmers' heads—which has become a popular tourist attraction (no. 227).

THE AMERICAS

181 A NATION OF ONIONS

Bermuda. "Onions" is the name given to the roughly sixty-five thousand inhabitants of Bermuda, and they even use it themselves. "The Onion Patch" is the nickname for the state comprising approximately three hundred sixty islands in the Atlantic Ocean. At one time the Bermuda onion, a slightly sweet vegetable imported from the Canary Islands, was their most important export and very popular, especially in the US. Today, they are no longer cultivated on the islands.

182 LIFESAVING ROOF CONSTRUCTION

Bermuda. The region is famed for its pink coral beaches, for the northernmost tropical coral in the world, for the Bermuda triangle (where ships and airplanes are said to disappear), and for its architecture: pastel-colored bungalow-like houses with typical white stone roofs. These roofs are vital for survival and are used to collect fresh rainwater, since the islands have no rivers or springs. They are shaped like stairs; each step forms a gutter, which channels the rain so that it can be collected.

183 JESUS AND THE KITES

Southampton. How do you explain the Ascension of Christ to children? Apparently, a teacher in Bermuda came up with the idea of drawing a portrait of Jesus on a kite and then flying it. It subsequently became an Easter custom: on Good Friday, hundreds of people fly their kites, many of which are homemade, on Horseshoe Bay Beach. It is a celebration, and the Gombey dancers appear in their colorful costumes.

184 THE SALUTATIONS OF JOHNNY FROM HAMILTON

Hamilton. Johnny Barnes (1923–2016) was unique. On weekday mornings, he used to spend a few hours standing on a roundabout in Hamilton, the capital of Bermuda, and greeting all the passersby. Waving, he would often add, "God loves you," and the Bermudians loved the old man. In 1998, a couple of traders joined together and donated a life-size sculpture of Johnny waving.

185 DON'T SLIP UP

The British Overseas Territory has gained a permanent place in the hall of fashion fame thanks to the "Bermuda shorts." And, of course, you can buy these men's shorts in all conceivable colors. However, when in town, shorts-wearers tend to go for pairs sporting golf patterns as leisurewear (Bermuda has the most golf courses per head in the world). And, if you need to look smart, simply pair the shorts with traditional shoes, knee-high socks, and a jacket and tie—surprisingly, it works!

186 GLACIER SHRINKAGE

Greenland. It is not only the biggest but also the iciest island in the world. About 85 percent of Greenland's 836,300 square miles (2.17 million square kilometers) is covered by a mountainous layer of ice, which is more than 1.9 miles (3 kilometers) thick in places. Each year, ten to fifteen thousand icebergs break away from this mass; the iceberg that hit the *Titanic* came from here. If Greenland's ice were to completely melt, the sea level would rise by an incredible 20 to 23 feet (6 to 7 meters).

187 SUMMER SOLSTICE IN THE FREEZING COLD

Greenland. Midsummer is the longest day of the year, on June 21, and is also celebrated in some Nordic countries. However, there is hardly a country that has more reason to celebrate than Greenland with its round-the-clock darkness in winter. It is but a small comfort that between May 25 and July 25 the sun never sets in Greenland, because it is only in July that temperatures rise above 32°F (0°C) in some parts of Greenland.

188 NO SOCCER WITHOUT GRASS

Greenland. A score of 16–0 against Sark was the Greenlandic soccer team's best-ever win, but there were also 0–6 losses against the Faroe Islands, Guernsey, and Minorca. Greenland plays international soccer without approval from FIFA. Soccer's world governing body has not accepted Greenland because it does not have a grass pitch. But now, artificial turf is allowed, and the island wants to have the same rights as the Faroe Islands, which is a member of FIFA.

189 THE LONGEST CANYON IN THE WORLD

Greenland. In 2013, researchers used ground-penetrating radar to discover the longest ravine in the world hidden under Greenland's ice. The "Grand Canyon of Greenland" measures at least 466 miles (750 kilometers) and is therefore significantly longer than the previous record holder, the Yarlung Tsangpo Canyon in Tibet, which measures approximately 310 miles (500 kilometers). However, the Tibetan canyon is a good 12.4 miles (20 kilometers) wide and a massive 19,685 feet (6,000 meters) deep. Greenland's is approximately 6 miles (10 kilometers) wide and 2,624 feet (800 meters) deep.

190 DON'T SLIP UP

The majority of Greenlanders are Kalaallit. Eskimo is a collective term for the (related) Arctic nations, which are also referred to as Inuit. The "Eskimo kiss" has become famous with people from modern Western cultures rubbing their noses against each other. The Eskimos, who call it *kunik*, only briefly touch noses and practice it only with relatives or close friends. A similar ritual is found among the New Zealand Maori and Asian peoples, who call it the "smell kiss."

191 AS STRONG AS A BEAR

Northwest Territories. The car license plates of the Canadian Northwest Territories are highly sought after among collectors. They show the outline of a polar bear—a design that was introduced in 1970 on the Arctic territory's hundredth anniversary. It is now a registered trademark.

192 MOVING DAY ON THE CALENDAR

Montreal. As a rental-car tourist, it is best to avoid Montreal on July 1. The official Moving Day in the province of Québec, known as *fête du déménagement* or *journée national du déménagement*, is the day when the vast majority of leases end, so those heading for a new home generally move on this day. In 2009, it involved more than 700,000 households in Québec.

193 IN THE WRONG PARLIAMENT

Montreal. On guided tours around Québec's parliament buildings in Montreal, the crests of Belgium and the Netherlands can be seen in the great hall. According to research, they must have found their way there between 1966 and 1975, but nobody knows why, and the donor is also unknown.

194 DON'T SLIP UP

Canada has successfully established itself as a multicultural country, so jokes about nationalities, religions, and languages are not appreciated. The only—domestic—exceptions were the Newfie jokes about Newfoundlanders (no, not the dogs), which have fallen out of fashion of late.

195 SUMMER SOLSTICE

USA. Painter and writer Elizabeth "Neal" Forsling, who lived on Casper Mountain in Wyoming, invited her girlfriends to celebrate Midsummer Eve each year. They came dressed as witches with pointed hats and told stories. The artist bequeathed her house and grounds to Wyoming, and it has become a museum and nature park. On Midsummer Eve, the tradition is still kept alive. A large bonfire is lit, and red earth is thrown on it to ensure happiness for the coming year.

196 WOMEN DRIVERS—BEWARE!

Memphis. This city in Tennessee is popular among hard-core Elvis fans. However, female fans (and other female tourists) should think twice before getting behind the wheel. According to an old law, somebody with a red flag should walk in front of a car driven by a woman, to warn pedestrians and other drivers. This law still exists today, at least on paper.

197 NAPOLEON AND THE FBI

Washington, DC. In 2017, the headquarters of the FBI in Washington, DC, acquired an attractive visitor center called the FBI Experience. However, the center is accessible only for US citizens (or valid green card holders) who have registered in advance. One of the things they can discover is who established the Federal Bureau of Investigation in 1908: it was Attorney General Charles Joseph Bonaparte, grandson of Napoleon's brother.

198 MONEY LAUNDERING

San Francisco. Money laundering in sight of an FBI office? In the tradition-steeped Westin St. Francis hotel on San Francisco's Union Square, money is flagrantly washed. A specially employed "coin washer" has been cleaning coins since the 1930s, when the ladies wore white gloves. Today, the shiny money is the trademark of the establishment.

199 DON'T SPOOK THE HORSES

New York City. There have been pushes to ban the horse-drawn carriages in Central Park, but if the popular attraction were to become a thing of the past, they would be missed by many tourists. Plus, an outdated law would become largely irrelevant: it is prohibited to put an umbrella up or down in the presence of a horse in the Big Apple.

200 DON'T SLIP UP

While the terminology is commonly used in other countries, don't ask where "the toilet" is when you're in the US. If you are looking for the bathroom, you can ask for the "restroom" or the "ladies' room" or "men's room." Women who want to be even more courteous go to the "powder room."

201 CHOCOLATE BARS INSTEAD OF JEANS

Cuilapa. The city in Guatemala is the geographical center of Central America, the land bridge between the two subcontinents. However, the country is not the birthplace of blue denim and instant coffee, although it is often claimed to be. The material for blue jeans comes from Nîmes in France, and instant coffee from New Zealand. However, chocolate bars may actually have been invented by the Mayans.

202 DELICIOUS FALL

Grenada. October 25, 1983, saw the commencement of an invasion by the US and neighboring islands. The action, which was disputed in international law, deposed the military junta. The American soldiers told the islanders about Thanksgiving, and subsequently many of them brought presents of turkey and cranberry sauce, which had been unfamiliar in Caribbean cuisine until then. Since then, Grenada has celebrated Thanksgiving.

203 DISAPPEARING FISH AND HANDICAPPED MONSTERS

Belize. Formerly known as British Honduras, Belize is home to heavenly Caribbean beaches. But on Good Friday, the locals do not go in the water, since they believe it will make all the fish disappear from Belize. The country's wealth of superstitions also warns against "El Sisimito," a human-eating monster with feet pointing backward and no knees, and a thumbless dwarf called "El Duende" who punishes any children who kill animals.

204 A VILLAGE AS THE CAPITAL

Belmopan. The capital of Belize, with just over twelve thousand inhabitants, is the smallest national capital in the world. It became the capital in 1961, when Hurricane Hattie almost destroyed Belize City, the capital at the time. Today, Belmopan and the rest of the country survive without a McDonald's, Burger King, Starbucks, and the like. Belize and Vatican City are the only countries in the world to go without such culinary delights. Incidentally, Belize's highest building is a 141-foot-high (43 meter) Mayan pyramid.

205 DON'T SLIP UP

With the exception of English-speaking Belize, the states of Central America all speak Spanish. However, it is generally a more formal language than that of the former Spanish colonial powers. You can shorten *buenos días* ("good morning"), *buenas tardes* ("good day"), and *buenas noches* ("good evening / good night") to *buenas*, but ¡*hola*! should be reserved for good friends. Older ladies and gentlemen also like to be addressed as *Doña* or *Don*, instead of *Señora* or *Señor*.

206 NOT RIGHT ON THE MONEY

Honduras. The national currency, the lempira, is named for a Lenca leader who died defending the country against the Spanish conquistadors. The lempira notes show a Native American, but not one from Honduras. It shows the leader of a North American tribe who probably never ventured so far south.

207 ONOMATOLOGY FOR EXPERTS

Honduras. The country owes its name to Christopher Columbus himself. The Spanish seafarer is often incorrectly described as the "discoverer" of the Americas (the Vikings were the first Europeans in the New World). Upon reaching the shores of Honduras after a storm, Columbus is said to have called out, "Thanks be to God that we have survived these depths"—the Spanish word for "depths" being *honduras*.

208 AMONG THE CHILDREN OF PIRATES

Bay Islands (Honduras). On these islands off the Caribbean coast live *catrachos* and *catrachas*, which is what male and female inhabitants of the islands call themselves. Blond hair and blue eyes are no rarity among them. Their northern European appearance is thanks to the British pirates, who established themselves on the islands in the seventeenth century. Allegedly one of them was the notorious Henry Morgan.

209 A GIANT'S MARBLES

Costa Rica. In the Diquis delta and on Isla del Caño in Costa Rica, you can find stone spheres weighing up to 16 tons, with a diameter of up to approximately 8 feet (2.4 meters). They are still a puzzle for academics, since it is unknown how they were formed. The famous stones even lured Indiana Jones to the Central American country; fortunately for Hollywood, he narrowly escapes one of these rolling stones in *Raiders of the Lost Ark*.

210 TREASURE ISLAND OFF RICH COAST

Cocos Island. The island, which lies just off Costa Rica ("rich coast") in the Pacific Ocean, is said to have been used by pirates as a place to hide their booty; Bennett Graham alone is said to have buried 7 tons of gold here. Even the "Treasure of Lima" is supposedly hidden beneath the island's soil, which has been dug up many times. However, the Cocos Island's true treasure is its beautiful nature, which is why Costa Rica has given it national park status.

211 FLAME THROWING IN HONOR OF THE VOLCANO

Najapa. "Like a snowball fight but hotter" is how one citizen described the Bolas de Fuego, a nighttime celebration on August 31 in Najapa, El Salvador, which remembers the eruption of El Playon volcano. At least one month in advance, people (mostly young folks) soak balls of rags in gas, which they then throw at each other as "fireballs" on the night of the celebration. Police and medics are on the scene.

212 CELEBRATE UNTIL THE RIND CRACKLES

El Salvador. Since 2005, the second Sunday in November has been the Día de las Pupusas in El Salvador. It is a national day in honor of the *pupusa*, a cornmeal flatbread. In 2007, the biggest-ever pupusa was made. The ingredients for this giant national dish: 440 pounds of cornmeal, 44 pounds of cheese, and 44 pounds of pork rinds and refried beans. Guinness World Records checked it out: the diameter was approximately 10 feet (3 meters).

213 A LAKE FULL OF BULLS

Lake Nicaragua. The origins of the freshwater sharks in Lake Nicaragua are not what was originally presumed. Researchers once believed that a volcano erupted and its lava formed a lake from what had once been a bay, but that is not the case. Rather, the bull sharks made their way to Nicaragua's biggest lake via the San Juan River. The "bulls of the ocean" also swim in other large lakes, such as the Zambezi.

214 ABOVE AND BELOW ALL THINGS

León. The huge cathedral of León (1860) in Nicaragua is the largest church in Central America and comes complete with underground chambers and crypts. From one of these chambers, seven tunnels lead to other churches. They were once intended as escape routes, especially from earthquakes. You can visit the tunnels—or go on the church roof; it is worth it for the beautiful view of the city and the surrounding area.

215 LEGENDARY BILLIONAIRE'S QUIRKS

Managua. In Nicaragua's capital city, Managua, if you stay at the Crowne Plaza Hotel and get a room on the top floor, you are following in the footsteps of a legendary eccentric hermit and germophobe. In 1972, millionaire Howard Hughes rented the top two floors of the Intercontinental Hotel, as it was known at the time. On his arrival, all staff had to wait in the basement because he did not want to be seen.

216 CREEPING COLLAPSE

Mexico City. Cracks in the street and scaffolding on buildings: visitors to the Mexican capital with twenty-four million inhabitants don't think anything of it. But Mexico City, which the Aztecs built on a lake island, is slowly sinking. It has sunk by around 33 feet (10 meters) over the last century. It is because the groundwater has been pumped dry for the city's water consumption and because the city is becoming heavier thanks to high-rise buildings. Nobody has an affordable solution.

217 BEETLES AND CORAL

Cancún. The VW Beetle was clearly a streamlined design. Proof of this is on display in the Caribbean current, in the form of a cement sculpture shaped like the iconic vehicle. It is found at a depth of 13 feet (4 meters) in artist Jason deCaires Taylor's underwater museum off the coast of Cancún. The car was manufactured in Mexico until 2012. The exhibit in the sea is intended to form the heart of a reef with other pieces.

218 EASTER TRADITIONS

Mexico. Easter fires are popular on all continents, either to banish the winter or to keep evil spirits at bay. In Mexico, images of Judas are burned (something that was once done throughout the Christian world). Many of these papier-mâché figures resemble unpopular politicians or other contemporaries. They are hung above the streets on Good Friday and burned on the Saturday. Mexico City has banned the ritual for being environmentally unfriendly, but the dolls continue to be made. Collectors like them.

219 STRANGE TREE DECORATION

Mexico City. In the canal neighborhood of Xochimilco, there is a very strange attraction. On the Isla de las Muñecas ("the Island of Dolls"), dolls rot in the trees. The now-deceased gardener Don Julián Santana, who blamed himself for a young girl drowning, hung them up over the years. Creepy!

220 DON'T SLIP UP ————— —————

Mexico's joyous cult of the dead, with plastic skeletons, grave parties, and decorated altars, is legendary. But if you are invited to somebody's home, you must pay close attention to the color of the bouquet that you give your host or hostess. Yellow flowers are used to show the deceased the way to freedom, and red ones hold dark magic. However, this dark magic can be allayed by combining the flowers with white blooms.

221 ECUADORIANS IN DISGUISE

Panama / Ecuador. Panama's most famous product, the Panama hat, does not actually originate from Panama but from Ecuador. When the Ecuadorians presented the French emperor Napoleon III with a hat, it was shipped from Panama, which caused the confusion. The headwear grew in popularity when President Theodore Roosevelt was pictured wearing an "original Panama hat" on a visit to the construction site of the Panama Canal.

222 NEW YEAR

Ecuador. In the final hour of the year, not only do Ecuadorians set off fireworks, but the results of many days' work go up in flames. The *monigotes*, life-size or larger-than-life figures made of papier-mâché, are burned. The majority are caricatures of politicians, captains of industry, or show-business stars. If a celebrity has annoyed you, simply make an effigy of them, paint it in bright colors, maybe stick a few firecrackers in their pockets, and then let it burn!

223 HUMAN WATERCRAFT

Panama Canal. The canal was expanded in 2016 in preparation for the expected competition from the planned Nicaragua canal. The work could mean that the toll prices could fall. It costs up to $400,000 for a cruise ship to pass, depending on weight. The lowest tariff was in 1928 for American swimmer Richard Halliburton, who weighed 150 pounds and paid $0.36. He was categorized as a "watercraft."

224 MEETING AL CAPONE FOR A DRINK

Panama Canal. Al Capone was the most famous owner of the luxury yacht *Santana*, which was built in 1912 for a Boston millionaire. Capone named her *Isla Morada* and used her to smuggle rum and other things from Cuba to Florida. Today, anyone can board the more modestly equipped vessel to make a journey that is still unusual: through the Panama Canal in just over eight hours. Naturally, there is alcohol on board.

225 NOAH'S ARK IN THE LAKE

Barro Colorado. Panama is one of the most biologically rich regions in the Americas. The Barro Colorado Island is of particular interest. When the Gatun Lake was flooded to create the Panama Canal, many animals fled to the island. In isolation (for a long time only researchers could access it), many rare exotic species were able to survive. Now, the Smithsonian Institute gives small groups guided tours through a part of the virgin forest.

226 FAILED HARVEST

Curaçao. The story behind the famous Blue Curaçao liqueur is one of huge success born out of failure. Attempts to grow the sweet Valencia orange trees on Curaçao produced only small inedible fruits. Fortunately, it was discovered that their skins could be used to distill a clear liqueur, which is generally colored blue, and the small island in the Caribbean became world famous.

227 PHOTOGRAPHING AIRPLANE BELLIES

Saint Martin. Sint Maarten, as the Dutch part of the island is known (the other half is French), has a deafening attraction. On Maho Beach, airplanes thunder past, just feet above bathers' heads, in order to land on the nearby runway. Many tourists head there to film the jets from below. A beach restaurant provides information on arrivals.

228 A BUCKET FOR THE SUPER RICH

St. Barts. A zinc-coated bucket is the prize for winning the Bucket Regatta, a race for large sailing yachts held in March off the exclusive island of St. Barts. The invitation-only event's participants are mainly millionaires, sometimes with great sporting ambitions. However, those who are grimly determined to win may be disqualified; the aim (as with its sister regatta in August in Newport) is "to win the party."

Like a pig in mud . . . or water: the pigs of Exuma in the Bahamas (no. 231).

229 WEEDS ON STRIKE

Antigua and Barbuda. The national flower of the small island state of Antigua and Barbuda is a yellow flowering species of agave, whose innards can also be used as fish bait. But more interestingly, they also have a national weed. "Widdy Widdy" (*Corchorus siliquosus*) has its own story. When the sugar cane workers went on strike in 1951 and consequently had no money, they fed themselves and their families from the perennial plant, which is a good source of protein when boiled.

230 KICK 'EM, JENNY!

Grenada. The "spice island," which supplies one-fifth of the global nutmeg harvest, owes its existence to a volcano that has long been dormant. Just a few miles north of the island, there is an active underwater volcano. The unusually named "Kick 'em, Jenny" most recently erupted in 2001. Fishing and tourist boats keep a respectful distance from the maritime fire mountain.

231 SWIMMING PIGS

Exuma. As soon as a tourist boat sails into the bay of Big Major Cay (the Bahamas), there is rustling from the bushes, and three or four pigs jump into the sea. Some of them paddle next to the boats and await their rations—for example, a cut-up melon or some bread. As soon as the food source dries up, they swim away. Locals say the pigs are the survivors of a shipwreck—or that they have just been tamed for tourists.

232 PROPHECY IN WHITE

Elbow Cay. In Hope Town on Elbow Cay in the Abacos Islands (the Bahamas), there is a graveyard for cholera victims. An epidemic arrived in the 1850s, probably from New York. The "White Lady of the Ridge" is also thought to be a cholera victim. According to the local legend, her ghost appears on the coast, and she looks out to see when a disaster is approaching.

233 A TREE'S INVIGORATING POWER

The Bahamas. The national tree of the Bahamas is called lignum vitae ("tree of life") in Latin. It was given this name because it was once used for medical purposes (and still is today, albeit to a lesser extent). German scholar and poet Ulrich von Hutten claimed to have been cured of syphilis with an extract from the tree. In general, the blue-flowering tree with extremely hard wood is thought to have an invigorating and aphrodisiac effect.

234 MUTATED OWLS

Andros. In the forests of the Andros Island, the mythical "chickcharnie" resides. It is a birdlike creature with three toes and red eyes. If locals spot it, they treat it well because it means good times are ahead. Also, something bad comes back to anyone who treats it badly. The legend may have a grain of truth in it: on Andros there was once an owl that somewhat resembled this description (of course, without the fantastical embellishments).

235 PIG PARADISE LOST

Paradise Island. Famous for its hotels, casinos, and rumors of alleged Mafia contacts, Paradise Island is connected by bridge to Nassau, the capital of the Bahamas. The tropical island, where many scenes from James Bond movies have been filmed, was once the second home of the rich and famous. However, before it could become glam, it had to change its name: it used to be called Hog Island.

236 MONEY FROM THE FIELD

Haiti. Haiti's currency is named after an ornamental pumpkin: the gourd. In the 1880s, the rulers on the north of the island declared that all calabashes were state property and collected them in order to use them as a replacement for money. Later, Haiti got coins and banknotes, but the old name stuck. Once the richest colony of France, Haiti is now one of the poorest countries in the world.

237 CHRISTMASTIME

On the tropical Cayman Islands, snow is only ever seen on TV. It is something that saddens many islanders, especially during Advent. Therefore, they have found a way to remedy it: on moonlit nights, the locals gather white sand from the beach. They scatter it around their houses and celebrate a "white Christmas." During these weeks, the snow gardens ensure a seasonal atmosphere in the often lavishly decorated houses.

238 NO MORE SMALL TALK WITH ALIENS

Arecibo. Puerto Rico's mountains were once the home of the largest spherical reflector radio telescope in the world, which filled a whole valley and had a diameter of 1,000 feet (305 meters) and a surface area covering 785,765 square feet (73,000 square meters). For years, the Arecibo Observatory sent out a radio signal that provided possible alien cultures with information about humans (it also appeared in several films, including 1995's James Bond film *GoldenEye*). Unfortunately, the telescope was damaged by Hurricane Maria in 2017 and then by earthquakes, and it ultimately collapsed in 2020.

239 THE LEGEND OF THE TAX HAVEN

Cayman Islands. The British Cayman Islands, the fifth largest banking center in the world, were a notorious tax haven. The legend that led to this dubious status: in 1794, ten ships were wrecked on the reef off Grand Cayman. The islanders managed to rescue nearly all passengers, including one of the king's relatives. Consequently, King George III waived all tax for the Caymans. Since no official documentation of this decree has ever been found, all evidence supporting this legend is anecdotal.

240 AN ISLAND BY ANY OTHER NAME

Dominica. The Caribbean island state of Dominica is often confused with the Dominican Republic, which is not too far away. Therefore, islanders have suggested reverting to the precolonial name of the island: Waitukubuli.

241 EXPENSIVE ISLANDS

Virgin Islands. The small Virgin Islands, today a duty-free shopping destination for American cruise tourists, were the most expensive land purchase Washington ever made. In 1917, it paid Denmark $26 million for the islands, which were used as a military base to protect the Panama Canal. In comparison, the Russian czar received only $7.2 million for Alaska in 1867.

242 THE TEN-DOLLAR MAN

Nevis. On Nevis, which forms a small country with Saint Kitts, a museum remembers Alexander Hamilton in the house of his birth. To date, he is the only person not born in the continental US to have appeared on a piece of United States paper currency. Hamilton was one of the founding fathers and the first US secretary of the treasury. Although he adorned the $10 bill in the US, he has yet to make it onto the currency of Saint Kitts and Nevis.

243 FARMED DELICACY

Providenciales. Conch chowder is a spicy Caribbean soup made from the meat of the large conch, which now adorns menus on the American Eastern Seaboard. Since the shells of many conch species were sought-after souvenirs, these marine animals had to be protected. Therefore, the first conch farm was established close to Providenciales on the Turks and Caicos Islands. It is a tourist attraction.

244 AN OFFSHOOT OFF GRENADA

The Grenadines. One of the most beautiful sailing spots in the Caribbean, the Grenadines certainly don't owe their name to the pomegranate, the fruit used to make grenadine syrup, which bartenders around the world use to turn cocktails a pretty red color. Rather, the chain of islands, which is part of the island state of Saint Vincent and the Grenadines, was named after the neighboring island state of Grenada, which presumably was given its name by Spanish seafarers from the city of Granada.

245 MEN OVERBOARD

Anguilla. Boat racing, or rather fishing boat regattas, is the sport of choice on Anguilla. "Every boat has its fans, every captain has his strategy, and every finish line has its exchange of words," say the Anguillians. The hundred-year-old tradition culminates in August with the Champion of Champions race. Just before reaching the finish line, crew members jump overboard in order to offload excess weight and make the boats faster for the final dash.

246 THE FESTIVAL OF THE LIMPING DEVIL

Dominican Republic. Hell breaks loose in the Dominican Republic in February, especially on the weekends. The colorfully clad *diablos cojuelos*, limping devils, take center stage and are allowed to hit anyone with balloons or small sandbags without fear of reprisal. Their devil-like masks are said to represent the facial expressions of the previous Spanish colonial rulers (*Perdón, Españoles!*).

247 VALUABLE BUGS

Puerto Plata. With a little bit of luck, you can find amber in the Dominican Republic. The petrified tree resin is sought after as jewelry, and collectors particularly like animals encased in it. One of the most famous pieces in the Amber Museum in Puerto Plata is the stone encasing a prehistoric mosquito that was seen in the film *Jurassic Park*.

248 OF DANCING AND OF KISSING

Dominican Republic. Merengue is the national music of the Dominican Republic and could be named after the egg white and sugar dessert, which is also known in Germany as *Baiser* (from the French word for "kiss"). The explanation suits the Caribbean style of music well, since churches have called for censorship of the rhythmic—and often very physical—dancing to occasionally X-rated lyrics. The efforts were unsuccessful; the merengue stayed and even became an export hit.

249 TRAVEL BACK IN TIME TO EUROPE

Altos de Chavón. The European Middle Ages can be found in the Dominican Republic. The small town of Altos de Chavón is the joint work of a Hollywood set designer and an American Austrian industrialist. The Greek amphitheater there does not quite fit with the history, but nevertheless it draws in the public. The church in the town was named for the patron saint of Poland, Saint Stanislaus, after a visit by Pope John Paul II.

250 FOR AND AGAINST (ALMOST) EVERYTHING

Dominican Republic. Mamajuana can fix almost everything; the people in the Dominican Republic are convinced of it. The unofficial national drink was developed from medicine used by the original inhabitants. Today, it is mainly mixed from red wine, rum, honey, herbs, and sometimes pickled woods. Then, as today, the brew was said to increase virality, although too much of a good thing is likely to cause pigheadedness.

251 THE HEADLESS EMPRESS

Fort-de-France. The capital of Martinique had a very strange tourist attraction: the beheaded statue (1856) of Empress Joséphine Bonaparte. Born in 1796 on Martinique as Marie Joséphe Rose de Tascher de la Pagerie, she married Napoleon. Today, she is still divisive in her homeland because she advocated the reintroduction of slavery. In 1991, her monument was beheaded. It was never repaired, and the statute was eventually torn down by activists in 2020.

252 ASHES FAR AND WIDE

Plymouth. There is not a soul living in the official capital of Montserrat, a British Overseas Territory. It was buried under thick ash when the Soufrière Hills volcano erupted in 1995. Since then, two-thirds of the island, including Plymouth, has been inaccessible due to poisonous gases. Little Bay, in the north of the island, is being established as a new capital, and a new airport is already in operation.

253 DELICIOUS, AT LEAST ONCE

Jamaica. The national dish, ackee and saltfish, must be cooked by well-versed chefs, because the fruit of the ackee tree is edible only when ripe. Unripe or overripe, the fruit is poisonous, and eating it could even be fatal. The fish served with it, usually cod, is fried in oil and chili. Captain William Bligh (known due to the mutiny on the *Bounty*) brought the first ackee plants to Kew Gardens in London.

254 EASTER TRADITIONS

Tobago. Goat races are almost as popular as cricket in the island state of Trinidad and Tobago. The Tuesday after Easter, known as Goat Race Day, is a de facto public holiday on Tobago. Thousands pile into the specially built stadiums in Buccoo and Mount Pleasant to watch the "jockeys" with long leashes chase after their trained racing goats. Nanny goats are generally quicker, while the billy goats can race for longer.

255 LACY PEAKS WITH PURPOSE

Saint Lucia. The women's national dress in Saint Lucia, which is called *madras* after a type of material, includes a head scarf that makes a statement. If one peak points out, it shows that the wearer is single; if two stick out, that she is married; and if three stick out, that she is a widow. And, unofficially, four tips means: "It doesn't matter, but talk to me." The official symbol of Saint Lucia is two peaks, which represent the Piton Mountains.

256 KENNEDY'S SUPPLY

Cuba. It's an old man's fantasy that cigars, Cuba's top souvenir, are rolled on the naked thighs of young Cuban women. Nevertheless, the island's tobacco product is highly regarded around the world, as proven by US president John F. Kennedy, who ordered 1,200 Cuban cigars in 1962, just a few hours before he signed a trade embargo with Cuba (which was slightly relaxed in 2015).

257 WHERE FREEDOM IS A SIN

Cuba. The Cuba Libre ("free Cuba") is one of the world's most popular cocktails and was doubtlessly inspired by American soldiers, who occupied Spanish Cuba after the 1898 Spanish-American war. Cuban exiles, aware that their country is run under a Communist dictatorship and is not free, sometimes call the rum and cola drink *mentirita* ("little lie").

258 JOHN LENNON WITHOUT THE GLASSES

Havana. In the 1960s and 1970s, the Beatles' music was subject to the anti-imperial ban in Cuba. However, in 2000, seventy-four-year-old Fidel Castro got a taste for it and had a monument to John Lennon erected in Havana. A bronze statue of the British star sits on a park bench. His glasses are often stolen, so a guard waits close by and puts the glasses on him for photos.

259 HOW RUM IS MADE FROM SUGAR

Cuba. After cigars, rum is the most popular souvenir from the Caribbean island. Before the Castro revolution, Cuba was the world's biggest sugar exporter, and correspondingly there is no lack of molasses, the basis for rum production. The sugar cane was brought over from Spain by Columbus on his second journey to the New World, but it is originally from the Far East.

260 DON'T SLIP UP

With the gradual relaxation of the American trade embargo against the Cuban government, the problem of toilet paper shortages on the island could be solved. Still, to avoid any unpleasant surprises (and the occasional unsavory public restroom), it's a good idea for visitors to pack a couple of packets of paper tissues in their suitcase. Incidentally, the toilet paper problem is not a good topic of conversation with proud Cubans, even if they are definitely aware of the shortage.

261 PAY PER DANCE

Buenos Aires. The neighboring country of Uruguay may well "outrageously" claim that it is the birthplace of tango, but all Argentinians know that Buenos Aires is the world capital of tango. For that reason, it hosts at least fifteen *milongas* or tango evenings each night. And there are at least as many "taxi dancers," skilled dancers that women seeking a tango partner can book relatively cheaply for an evening at the dance hall.

262 THE GIRL WHO DIED TWICE

Buenos Aires. The Cementerio de la Recoleta in Buenos Aires is not only the last place of rest for many poets and presidents, but it is also a tourist attraction. Many visitors head for the grave of Eva Perón. By contrast, the grave of "the girl who died twice" is unsettling. Rufina Cambaceres was mistakenly buried alive in 1902. She managed to free herself, but on the way out of the cemetery, she died of a heart attack.

263 THE LONG WAY TO USHUAIA

Ushuaia. The city located on the island of Isla Grande de Tierra del Fuego not only is the "Gateway to Antarctica" (the majority of cruises start there) but is also classified as the southernmost city in the world. However, Ushuaia is not connected by land to the rest of Argentina. If you are traveling by car, you must drive through Chile. This border was subject to a conflict where both sides threatened the use of arms. It was only in 1978 that Pope John Paul II was able to defuse the situation.

264 SMALL TOWN IN A SALT CRUST

Villa Epecuén. Villa Epecuén in the province of Buenos Aires is a strange attraction. The small town on a very salty lake made a good living from health tourism until 1985, when the lake dam burst and Villa Epecuén was submerged under approximately 33 feet (10 meters) of water. The water has been receding since 2010, and the town now appears like a salt-encrusted modern Pompeii. Visitors are returning to see the ruins.

The Beatles ruled the
pop charts in the 1960s.
Decades later, even
Fidel Castro admitted to
being a Beatles fan and
had this John Lennon
statue erected in
Havana (no. 258).

265 DON'T SLIP UP

Argentinians of both sexes, particularly in Buenos Aires, place great importance on elegance. If you don't want to draw negative attention to yourself, take care of your personal hygiene and clothing. Away from the backpacker scene, you should change to a different shirt or blouse in the evening. And on the beaches, scruffy trunks are an object of occasionally overt ridicule. Women's beach clothing should generally follow the demure but erotic style: show little but imply a lot.

266 LEGAL COKE

La Paz. At 10,500 to 13,450 feet (3,200 to 4,100 meters) above sea level, Bolivia boasts the highest capital city in the world. As a drug against altitude sickness, many of the locals chew the leaves of the coca plant, which contains a low (and legal) dose of cocaine. Coca-Cola once processed tons of the leaves. Without cocaine, but with specially trained pilots, airplanes approach the highest international airport in La Paz.

267 GOATS FOR DOMESTIC BLISS

La Paz. At the Mercado de Brujas, the "witches' market," you can buy nearly everything that is needed for the occult magic of the Indigenous Aymara people: amulets, mysterious tinctures, special herbs, and magic equipment. Goats' feet are a bestseller because they supposedly bring luck if you bury them in the foundations of a new house.

268 BY BIKE ON THE ROAD OF DEATH

La Paz / Coroico. Certainly the most dangerous stretch in the world, the approximately 40-mile-long (65 kilometer) "Road of Death" takes you from La Paz to Coroico through the Yungas mountains. On the tracks cut into the slopes, vehicles drive on the left-hand side for additional safety, despite Bolivia otherwise being a right-hand side driving country. There used to be two to three hundred deaths per year on this road. Since 2007, a stretch has been made safer. Today, only bicycle tourists use the old route.

At the Mercado de Brujas in La Paz, you can find everything a good witch needs, even goats' feet (no. 267).

269 SAILORS WITHOUT THE SEA

Bolivia. Why does a landlocked country need naval officers and sailors? Bolivia needs them for two reasons. First, the "naval force" watches for drug smugglers on the rivers and also along the border to Peru, which runs across Lake Titicaca in the Andes. Second, the marines are essentially a living reminder that Bolivia demands the return of its access to the Pacific: a 248-mile (400 kilometer) coastline that it lost to Chile in the 1883 war.

270 BEDDED IN SALT

Salar de Uyuni. The world's largest salt flat at 11,985 feet (3,653 meters) above ground is quickly becoming an international tourist attraction. Tours of part of the 113,904-square-foot (10,582 square meter) playa often lead to Incahuasi Island, with its giant Trichocereus cacti and also to a "train cemetery." Tourists like staying in one of the hotels that are constructed entirely from salt.

271 THE PERFECT (RIVER) WAVE

Amazon River. *Pororoca* means "great roar," and the biggest tidal bore in the world does this name justice. It generally occurs only twice a year, in February and March, when the Atlantic surges so powerfully up the Amazon River and its adjacent rivers that waves of up to 13 feet (4 meters) in height travel up to approximately 75 miles (120 kilometers) inland. It makes for an amazing experience for surfers, but not one wholly without danger. The record on a surfboard is thirty-seven minutes, covering a distance of approximately 8 miles (12.5 kilometers).

272 THE LONGEST BEACH IN THE WORLD

Rio Grande / Chuí. The best choice for long beach walks—and we mean really long—is the Cassino Beach in Brazil. The longest beach in the world measures 158 miles (254 kilometers) and stretches from the mouth of the Rio Grande to the mouth of the Chuí on the border with Brazil's southern neighbor, Uruguay. The uninterrupted coastline is approximately 62 miles (100 kilometers) longer than the beach at the no. 2 spot: the Ninety Mile Beach in the Australian state of Victoria.

273 KILLERS IN THE PAN

Piranhas. Piranhas in Piranhas? It's true. For example, at the Badaué restaurant, the predatory fish is fried in oil and a little salt. The pretty colonial town, whose citizens get paint to decorate their houses every year, is relaxed about its unusual name, even though *piranha* can also mean "prostitute."

274 GERMAN CELEBRATIONS IN BRAZIL

Blumenau. Blumenau's Oktoberfest, with 600,000 visitors, is only the fifth biggest in the world (behind Germany's Munich with six million visitors, Qingdao in China with three million, Germany's Hanover with one million, and Kitchener in Canada with 700,000). However, the town—established by German pharmacist Hermann Blumenau—hosts the second biggest public event in Brazil, after the carnival in Rio de Janeiro. The beer and samba party has been held since 1984.

275 DON'T SLIP UP

"Girls from Ipanema" or even other beaches in Brazil wear the smallest bikinis in the world. However, going topless is frowned upon and can lead to an expensive encounter with the police. But, since 2014, Rio has had an official nudist beach at Praia do Abrico. However, Balneário Camboriú—a large beach resort city—beat them to it; its Praia do Pinho has been a naturist beach since 1987. Men who are not accompanied by a woman may not enter.

276 A TRUE INFINITY POOL

Algarrobo. Sailing in the pool? Not a problem in the Chilean holiday complex San Alfonso del Mar. The guaranteed shark-free pool is over 0.62 miles (1 kilometer) long and sits on just over 19 acres (7.7 hectares) right next to the Pacific. But the world's biggest swimming pool to date is currently facing some competition, since a larger pool is under construction in Egypt.

The largest salt flat in the world is the final resting place for old trains (no. 270).

277 A LONG WAY TO CITY HALL

Valparaíso. As the seat of parliament and "Chile's cultural capital," Valparaíso boasts a UNESCO World Heritage Site in its old town. It also holds the dubious title of the "most sprawling urban area in the world." The Desventuradas Islands, located about 684 miles (1,100 kilometers) off the coast, are within the city limits, although only a small army unit lives on the rocks.

278 KISSES FOR BIG FOOT

Punta Arenas. Chile's southernmost city and the starting point for journeys to Cape Horn is located on the Strait of Magellan, discovered in 1520 by Ferdinand Magellan. The central monument in the town is dedicated to him. At his feet sits a Native American made of bronze. Stroking the foot of this Patagonian (literally "big foot") brings luck, and kissing it ensures a return visit to Punta Arenas.

279 THE ORIGIN OF THE TAPATI FESTIVAL

Easter Island. Racing down an extinct volcano crater on a banana trunk sled is not without danger. But this highlight of the Tapati Festival on Easter Island is derived from the tradition of a much more dangerous sport. Long ago, the islanders competed to collect bird eggs from a rock in the sea, where many were attacked by sharks. Today, the challenges are different, but the victor is still the uncrowned king of the island.

280 DON'T SLIP UP ————— —————

In Chile, it is considered very inappropriate to bring red flowers as a hostess gift, because they symbolize death. Yellow roses are also not a good choice, since they are understood as a sign of contempt. And a particular tip for the Swiss, who like to give their famous army knives to their hosts: in Chile, any kind of blade is regarded as a symbol of separation.

281 CLOSE ENOUGH TO TOUCH THE STARS

The Andes. No other country is as close to the universe as Ecuador. This is true even though Mount Everest in Asia is 29,032 feet (8,849 meters) high and Mount Chimborazo in Ecuador is much lower at 20,564 feet (6,268 meters). The solution to the puzzle: Ecuador is on the equator, and because the world bulges out more than 12 miles (20 kilometers) around its middle, Chimborazo's summit is much closer to the sun, moon, and stars than its competitor in the Himalayas.

282 MILITARY BASE WITHOUT MILITARY

Tiwintza. Ecuador and Peru have often fought border wars, which were settled only in 1999 with a "protocol." Part of the agreement was to cede approximately 0.4 square miles (1 square kilometer) of Peru, a former Ecuadorian military base, to Ecuador. However, military use is prohibited, and Ecuador has no sovereign rights. This mountainous piece of land will become a jointly administered national park.

283 NO COUNTRY FOR OLD MEN

Vilcabamba. Many 110-, 120-, and even 130-year-olds live in Vilcabamba. In the so-called valley of longevity, it looks like they have discovered eternal life. The valley has become a regional tourist destination, and esotericists believe the "heart of the world" is there. However, it's all just fibs, since scientists have found that Vilcabamba has a normal mortality rate. But the tourists still come—you never know!

284 VAMPIRES ON THE GALÁPAGOS ISLANDS

Galápagos Islands. The vampire finch is found on only two tiny, uninhabited Galápagos Islands, one named for Charles Darwin and the other for Theodor Wolf, a German theologist and geologist. The unusual species of bird gets its name from its diet: it feeds primarily on the blood of other birds. It is particularly fond of the blue-footed boobie, picking skin off the much larger bird to get at its blood.

285 DON'T SLIP UP

Invited to someone's home for dinner in Ecuador? Then make yourself popular by offering to set the table, if there is no help. The same goes for clearing the table after highly praising the meal. However, you should also leave a clean plate, because uneaten food is seen as a criticism. You will also make your host happy if you participate in the usually animated table talk: sports and the Galápagos Islands are good topics.

286 GIANT "BOAT" FOR CHILDREN

Guyana. The county achieved world fame only once: in 1978, when members from a San Francisco–based cult committed mass suicide in a remote settlement in Guyana, resulting in more than nine hundred fatalities. Yet, the tiny state in northeastern South America is a friendly country. This friendliness is symbolized by its national flower, upon whose leaves a child can safely sit. The round leaves of the *Victoria amazonica* water lily can reach a diameter of nearly 10 feet (3 meters).

287 BALANCING ACT AS THE NATIONAL SPORT

Paraguay. The country has two national dances: the polka, which came to the country with the many German-speaking Mennonites, and the unique bottle dance. Young women balance on their heads at least one bottle decorated in the national colors. Well-practiced dancers combine this balancing act with artistic floorwork.

288 DUTCH WITH LOCAL COLOR

Suriname. Suriname is the only country in South America where Dutch has been officially spoken since colonial times. However, the language is sometimes intermingled with a type of local slang. And so *Waar kan ik pinnen?* is just asking where the ATM is. The word *bombel*, for "firework," is important because according to the locals, Suriname holds the record for the most fireworks per capita (approximately 540,000 inhabitants).

289 RED AND WHITE GLOBAL SUCCESS

Colombia. At some point, someone somewhere in Colombia had the idea of mixing tomato ketchup and mayo, adding a little lime juice and a few drops of tabasco. That was how *salsa rosada* was created. It became a kitchen favorite first in Colombia and then in the neighboring countries. Since then, it has spread around the world and is known as cocktail sauce.

290 NEW YEAR

Colombia. Traveling is a New Year's resolution in many countries, in particular in Colombia, where the inhabitants run around their homes with empty suitcases. That is not the only custom: if you eat lentils at the start of the year, you will not go hungry. The custom of red underwear has been imported from Spain, but with a local variation: yellow underwear is said to ensure wealth. And to be extra sure, Colombians hold money in their hands as the clock strikes twelve.

291 EXTRA DRY

Lima. "It never rains in Southern California" is a well-known pop music claim that many tourists discover is not true. But in Lima, the capital of Peru and the third biggest city in the Americas after São Paulo and Mexico City, the saying is as good as true. Thanks to the combination of a warm desert climate and the cold Humboldt Current, it rains only a little in the winter months (July to September), even though the sky is gray for weeks on end.

292 THE HIGHEST DUNE IN THE WORLD

Nazca. Among the mountains of the Andes, the highest dune in the world towers close to the city of Nazca, famous for its mysterious geoglyphs. The 3,828-foot-high (1,167 meter) sand mountain is perfect for a downhill run of up to 1,968 feet (600 meters) on a specially made "sandboard." However, before the thrill, you must make the strenuous three-hour ascent, because this sand monster is approximately 6,847 feet (2,078 meters) above sea level.

293 OUT-OF-THE-WAY CHASM

The Andes. Even if patriotic Peruvians like to claim so, the deepest canyon in the world is not the 11,004-foot-deep (3,354 meter) Cotahuasi Canyon in the Andes. However, it is the deepest chasm in the Americas; the world-famous Grand Canyon in Arizona is only approximately 5,905 feet (1,800 meters) deep. In order to reach Cotahuasi Canyon, you have to endure a ten-to-twelve-hour bus journey primarily on dirt roads.

294 NEW YEAR'S RITES

Peru. New Year in Peru is a riot of yellow—particularly new yellow underwear. It has to be put on before midnight (even over your clothes) and is a popular holiday present among friends to bring luck. As in Colombia, those who want to travel in the coming year will run around with an empty suitcase when the clock strikes twelve, and those seeking financial happiness count their *nuevo sol* or money in the night.

295 DON'T SLIP UP

In Peru, if someone you know links arms with you, then you have gained a friend, because this gesture is normal with good acquaintances (and among friends). However, if a complete stranger makes contact with you in that way, be aware. He has recognized you as a *gringo* and likely wants your money. Another way to slip up: calling the Indigenous people of Peru "Indians" is extremely impolite.

296 ORIENTAL ONOMASTICS

Uruguay. The official name of Uruguay is the "Oriental Republic of Uruguay," which is why its citizens also poetically call themselves Orientals. The name refers to the location of the country in the east of South America. Uruguay has a population of 3.4 million, but there are three times as many cattle and sheep. The capital, Montevideo, is named in honor of its 433-foot-high (132 meter) hill (*monte* is Latin for "mountain"), which Magellan wrote of in his logbook in 1520.

297 THE LONGEST NATIONAL ANTHEM IN THE WORLD

Uruguay. Orientales, la patria o la tumba! "Orientals, our nation or the grave!" So goes the first line of the longest national anthem in the world, which belongs to Uruguay and features a staggering fourteen verses. Generally, only the first verse plus the chorus is sung. However, at a qualification match for the soccer World Cup in Costa Rica, the singer belted out the full anthem (against FIFA regulations for a ninety-second performance). The referee wanted to interrupt him, but the Uruguayan team threatened to "rip his head off."

298 URUGUAYAN INDULGENCE

Uruguay. *Chivito*, the national dish of Uruguay, is not exactly diet friendly. Between two slices of bread, you will find a slice of beef fillet, a slice of mozzarella, a fried egg (or a hardboiled egg cut into slices), at least one slice of bacon, tomatoes, olives, and occasionally even cucumber. Then the whole thing is served with mayo and a portion of fries!

299 DUELING NOW PROHIBITED

Uruguay. The country, which is today one of the safest and most peaceful in South America, was notorious in the last century for its men's enthusiasm for dueling. In order to better regulate these battles of honor, in 1920 the government issued a law to make dueling legal. The law remained in force until modern times, and it was only in 1992 that dueling was prohibited. However, prior to that it had largely fallen out of favor.

300 BEND IT LIKE BECKHAM

Uruguay. The Uruguayans also consider soccer matches against England as a duel, and the feeling is mutual. British railway workers first taught the Uruguayans how to kick a ball properly, with so much success that the "motherland of football" gained a feared rival. In 1930, Uruguay held the first FIFA World Cup for soccer and won the final against Argentina. England did not enter.

Reading and swimming at the same time—a typical thing to do in the Dead Sea (no. 309).

MIDDLE EAST

301 PUTTING RELIGION UP THE FLAGPOLE

Iran. Iran's flag has more written characters than any other national flag, although the untrained eye can barely see it. The shapes in the central horizontal white stripe symbolize a tulip, which together form the word *Allah* ("God"). The upper green and the lower red stripe merge into the central white stripes through the white writing. Each border bears the script *Allahu Akbar* ("God is great").

302 BEWARE OF CROCODILES

Iran. You occasionally come across crocodiles in Sistan and Baluchestan Province. They are mugger crocodiles, which are widespread on the Indian subcontinent. Capable of growing up to approximately 13 feet (4 meters) long, they even hunt on land at night. After a long drought in the 1990s they were endangered, but a heavy storm saved their habitat, enabling dried-out waters to flow again. Keep your eyes peeled!

303 QUICKY MARRIAGES

Iran. Fancy being married for just a couple of hours? That is not a problem in Iran, of all places. The *sigheh* process allows Muslims to enter into fixed-term marriage contracts. Critics see it as a form of permitting otherwise-prohibited prostitution, while its advocates maintain that it gives children born out of wedlock rights and suggest that divorced women have better chances of marrying again than unmarried women who are no longer virgins. There is even a *sigheh* consultation service on the internet.

304 MISTAKE IN THE CARPET

Tehran. Iran is still regarded as producing the best rugs, even though "real Persian rugs" are no longer as popular as they were in our grandparents' era. The Carpet Museum of Iran in Tehran shows off this art form. It provides courses in carpet weaving and design and runs a repair workshop. Incidentally, in the past, devout weavers intentionally worked small, almost invisible mistakes into their work, because only Allah can be perfect.

305 DON'T SLIP UP

In the theocracy of Iran, in addition to the prohibition of alcohol, similar to many Muslim countries, there are also regulations regarding clothing. For example, bright colors are not recommended for either women or men, and men's shorts are taboo. When entering Iran, women should ensure that no skin is visible except their face and hands. A headscarf must cover their hair, even though young women, especially in Tehran, like to show a little more than the hairline or even wear see-through scarfs.

306 A ZOO WITHOUT PIGS

Jerusalem. "This is not a pig" is written above the enclosure of the Chacoan peccary at the Jerusalem Biblical Zoo. The sign is there because pigs are considered unclean both for Muslims and Jews. In the Bible there is no mention of the Chacoan peccary, but that is also the case for other animals in this zoo. Ultimately, they all are examples of divine creation. Of the 130 animals named in the Bible, many live in this zoo if they are not extinct.

307 FREE READING ON THE BEACH

Tel Aviv. Among other things, the city is famous for its beaches. However, sunshine can quickly get boring if you forget your beach reading at the hotel. Not a problem here; the municipality's cultural department has set up mobile beach libraries, which everyone can use free of charge. There are books in Hebrew, Arabic, Russian, French, and English, and even some for children.

308 REPORTING FOR DUTY ON VACATION

Israel. Tourists can report for duty with the Israeli armed forces for a few days. The volunteers wear the uniform of the army, but they do not bear arms. They are given board and lodging but no pay. However, there is a cultural program. The concept came about during the 1982 Lebanon War; at the time, it was a serious idea but is now just an unusual vacation.

309 SALT OF THE EARTH

Dead Sea. Skin problems can be cured in the Dead Sea, and you can bathe and read at the same time—an image snapped by many a tourist. The salt content of the water is so high that you cannot sink. It is not a surprise because the water is 28 percent salt. There are a few lakes that have more salt—the saltiest, at 39 percent salt, being Lake Retba in Senegal, once the finishing line of the Dakar Rally.

310 DON'T SLIP UP

Jews observe a strict Sabbath day of rest, which often has complicated rules that frequently confuse foreigners. Be aware that the Sabbath starts on Friday evening and is therefore longer than just Saturday. In a hotel, you should ask for a room on the lower floors, because elevators are often switched off. High-rise hotels often have Sabbath elevators that do not require operation because they stop on every floor. In many hotels, you cannot check in or out during the Sabbath.

311 THE BEST VIEW OF THE "PROMISED LAND"

Abarim Mountains. Devout Jews believe Moses's burial site is on Mount Nebo. For Moses, who led the Jews from Egyptian captivity, a prophecy came true at the summit. God had told him that he would see the Promised Land but would not set foot there. The 2,650-foot-high (808 meter) mountain is in fact a good vantage point to see Israel. In 393 CE, a church was built there.

312 CLEAN WATER? NO THANK YOU!

Jordan. The baptism site of Jesus in the Jordan Valley is a special place of pilgrimage. However, because the river is often just a trickle due to water abstraction, Jordan has created baptism sites close by. Many pilgrims don't use them because they want the "original" experience and prefer to use the brown brook.

313 "PHILLY" IN THE MIDDLE EAST

Amman. During tours of the Jordanian capital, tourists from the US are often surprised because there is a lot of talk about Philadelphia. It is Jordan's fifth biggest city and former capital (1790–1800). Are the towns twinned? No, the name is historical. Under Ptolemaic rule, King Ptolemy II Philadelphus named the city on seven hills after himself, a name that remained for almost nine hundred years.

314 TREASURE IN THE BURIAL CHAMBER

Petra. Jordan's tourism highlight is Petra ("rocks"), whose buildings were hewn directly into the red stone. Petra can be reached through a narrow gorge (*siq* in Jordanian Arabic), which increases the visual impact of the buildings. The most famous façade is part of the incorrectly named "Treasury of the Pharaoh," which was once a funerary temple. According to the legend, this is where Moses struck water out of rock.

Almost like Jesus's time: a baptism ceremony in the Jordan (no. 312)

315 PETRA AND THE "QUEEN OF CRIME"

Petra. Without a doubt, Agatha Christie was a true fan of Petra. She often traveled to the Middle East with her husband, a famous archeologist, and was so enchanted by Petra that she set one of her crime novels there. In it, a sadistic woman is murdered and Hercule Poirot solves the case in record time. *Appointment with Death* has been filmed several times.

316 HARRY POTTER STRICTLY FORBIDDEN

Saudi Arabia. If you are traveling to Saudi Arabia to visit friends with children, you would do best to leave Harry Potter books and DVDs at home. The British junior wizard, like anything else that is loosely associated with "witchcraft," is banned. Famously, alcohol is also prohibited, leading to the creation of *siddique*, the illegally home-distilled alcohol whose name means "little friend." Incidentally, the word "alcohol" originates from Arabic.

317 WOMEN-ONLY LINGERIE SHOPS

Saudi Arabia. Sexy underwear has created a Catch-22 situation in the country, where women do not enjoy many rights. Women may only be homemakers, yet it does not sit well with the orthodox morals that sales assistants—men not from their family—show underwear to women. Upon the urgence of women, the Saudi monarchy ultimately decided that women may work in lingerie shops, but the entire staff must be female. It caused protests by the devout.

318 THE HIGHEST BUILDING IN THE WORLD

Jeddah. In Jeddah, the Saudi monarchy has commissioned the construction of Jeddah Tower (formerly called Kingdom Tower), which would be the largest building in the world at 3,304 feet (1,007 meters) tall. Construction on the project began in 2013 but then was put on hold. Plans call for the tower to comprise offices, apartments, and a hotel. The highest viewing platform in the world will be built at 1,647 feet (502 meters). Initially, the building was intended to be 1 mile high (1,600 meters), but engineers say that only 1 kilometer (0.62 miles) is currently possible.

319 CAR SURFING

Saudi Arabia. For many Saudi Arabian young men, money is not a problem. However, there are limited opportunities to spend it for enjoyment, which could be the reason that a new "sport" has developed. It involves 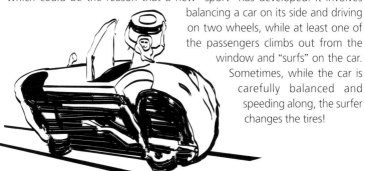 balancing a car on its side and driving on two wheels, while at least one of the passengers climbs out from the window and "surfs" on the car. Sometimes, while the car is carefully balanced and speeding along, the surfer changes the tires!

320 DON'T SLIP UP

The Islamic fundamentalist state of Saudi Arabia can still be a tricky destination for female tourists. Even business trips pose difficulties for women. Local women lead a regulated life in public, and the same is expected of foreign women. Therefore, women may need to wear headscarves, and figure-concealing clothing is recommended.

321 SPONSORED BY KHALIFA

Dubai. At 2,716 feet (828 meters) high, the biggest building in the world is the Burj Khalifa in Dubai. The tower, which opened in 2010, was to be called Burj Dubai. But when the global financial crisis sent the seemingly endlessly rich Dubai into monetary turmoil, Sheikh Khalifa from the United Arab Emirates provided a loan worth billions. Since then, the building has been called Burj Khalifa in honor of the rich donor.

Anything Pisa can do, Abu Dhabi can do better (no. 322)!

322 MORE LEANING THAN THE LEANING TOWER

Abu Dhabi. Forget Pisa. The most lopsided tower in the world is no longer in Italy. There are several other towers that lean more, including a church tower in Germany. The world-record leaning tower is found in Abu Dhabi, the capital of the United Arab Emirates. The Capital Gate skyscraper (525 feet or 160 meters) has an intentional lean of 18 degrees, and its upper floors are a luxurious hotel.

323 MILLIONS FOR NUMBER ONE

Abu Dhabi. In Abu Dhabi, in addition to admiring the many luxury cars on the streets, a look at the registration plates can also be interesting. In some cases, the registration plate is more expressive than the fancy vehicle it is attached to. The United Arab Emirates auctions off special numbers for charity. The most expensive registration plate shows the number 1. It was won by a businessman in 2008 at a cost of 55.2 million dirham ($14 million).

324 THE "GREENEST" CITY IN THE WORLD

Abu Dhabi. Surprisingly, it is the oil-rich Abu Dhabi that has built the first city in the world to be powered by renewable energy. The largely car-free Masdar City was designed to be home to about 48,000 inhabitants and 1,500 companies by 2025. Drinking water will come from solar-powered seawater desalination plants. The neighboring international airport is naturally located outside the "green" city.

325 ART ATTRACTS ART

Abu Dhabi. A visit to the Louvre and the Guggenheim on the same day? It was at least theoretically possible in the days of the Concorde airplane, which commuted at supersonic speed between Paris and New York. Soon it will be possible again . . . in Abu Dhabi. The Louvre has already opened a branch there. However, construction on the spectacular Frank Gehry–designed building for the Guggenheim has been delayed.

The golden rock on Mount Kyaiktiyo is covered in gold leaf. According to the legend, it is held in place only by a single strand of Buddha's hair (no. 397).

ASIA

326 THE DEAD GOAT GAME

Afghanistan. Although the country would like to see its national sport, *buzkashi*, at the Olympics, the chances of it being admitted are rather low because it uses a dead goat as sports equipment. To boot, the sport is considered dangerous. One team on horseback has to transport the goat's carcass to a circle drawn in chalk in the opposition's half, while the other side, which is also mounted, tries with all their might to grab it.

327 POLITICS ON THE MOUNTAIN

Tajikistan. The highest mountain in the country, the 24,589-foot-high (7,495 meter) Ismoil Somoni Peak in the Pamir Mountains is named for a Samanid emir who ruled between 897 and 907. However, the mountain has also had a "political career." During the Soviet era, when Tajikistan was part of the USSR, the mountain was first named for Stalin, and then it was called "Communist Peak." There is also a rumor that Russian soldiers encountered a yeti on the mountain.

328 FREE HEATING AS A NATIONAL HOBBY

Turkmenistan. If you are invited to someone's home, you will never freeze, even when the outside temperatures are low. Turkmenistan, which is rich in oil and gas, provides its citizens with free gas and electricity. Therefore, many Turkmen leave their heating on around the clock, from fall to the start of summer. The insider joke is that they are saving on matches, which are used to reignite the gas heating.

329 NO BEACH IN SIGHT

Uzbekistan. With the exception of the small Alpine state of Liechtenstein, Uzbekistan is the only country on Earth that is "double land-locked," meaning that it is surrounded by other land-locked countries. In a clockwise direction starting from the west, Uzbekistan's neighbors are Kazakhstan, Kyrgyzstan, Tajikistan, Afghanistan, and finally Turkmenistan (Liechtenstein is surrounded by Switzerland and Austria).

330 THE "STAN" COUNTRIES

The Silk Road. The seven states along the ancient silk road whose names end in "stan" are often simply called the "Stan" countries in international political jargon. The most well-known are Pakistan and Afghanistan. The affix "stan"—which comes from Persian—means "home of," such as "home of the Afghans." In addition, there are also many regions whose names end in the same way; for instance, Kurdistan in the Middle East.

331 ANTHEMIC NOBEL POET

Bangladesh / India. The neighboring countries of Bangladesh and India generally have a good, albeit occasionally adversarial, relationship with each other. They are also united by an unusual similarity: Bengali poet Rabindranath Tagore, who was born in India, wrote the lyrics to both the Bangladeshi and the Indian national anthems. The words come from two different poems by the poet, who in 1913 was the first person from Asia to receive a Nobel Prize.

332 DISPUTE ABOUT A GHOST ISLAND

South Talpatti / New Moore Island. Bangladesh and India strongly disputed a rock island that emerged in the Bay of Bengal after a cyclone. Both countries laid claim to the new island, measuring 2.17 miles (3.5 kilometers) long and 1.86 miles (3 kilometers) wide. Bangladesh called it South Talpatti, and India called it New Moore Island or Purbasha. Nature put an end to the dispute in its own unique way: in 2010, the island was again taken by the sea.

333 CIVILIZED FIGHTING

Bangladesh. *Kabaddi* is a ball sport originally from India that developed from military training. Its objective is to gain territory. In 1972, the regulated jostling became the national sport of Bangladesh, and a version without rules has the beautiful name *ha du*. Despite the best efforts of the Bangladeshi government in favor of *kabaddi*, the most popular sport in Bangladesh remains cricket.

334 WHO IS GOING TO READ ALL OF THAT?

Bangladesh. A glance at the newsstand in the cities of Bangladesh will amaze you on account of the multitude of publications. According to estimates by experts, there are approximately two thousand weekly or monthly magazines and daily newspapers. With a population of approximately 157 million, this number would not be unusual, but it is surprising in light of the low purchasing power and an illiteracy rate of around 42 percent.

335 THE COUNTRY OF SIX SEASONS

Bangladesh. Most countries in the world have four seasons, while some tropical countries have only two: the dry season and the rainy season. But Bangladesh has a total of six seasons: *bosonto* or spring, *grishmo* or summer, *borsha* or the rainy season, *shorot* or fall, *hemonto* or the cool season, and finally *sheeth* or winter. So it's no surprise that Bangladeshis also call their homeland the "playground of the seasons."

336 HAPPINESS AROUND EVERY CORNER

Bhutan. This country is unlike many other states, because the most important measure is not the gross domestic product but the "gross national happiness" index. It is based on four pillars: sustainable development, protection of the environment, preservation of national cultures, and good governance. However, your happiness will plummet if you kill an animal from a protected species, since the sentence of that crime in the Himalayan kingdom is life imprisonment.

337 PLEASE NO TRAFFIC LIGHTS

Thimphu. Bhutan is one of the few countries in the world that gets along fine without traffic lights. Thimphu, the capital boasting a respectable 80,000 inhabitants, used to have a set of lights, but the citizens made it clear to the government that they did not want the newfangled signals. The traffic lights were mothballed, and since then police in white gloves have once again been directing the traffic.

338 FIERCE DRAGONS

Bhutan. The locals call Bhutan *Druk Yul*, which means land of the thunder dragons. The name is inspired by the thundering storms that rage over the Himalayas. The dragon also features on their orange-yellow national flag. At approximately 14,672 square miles (38,000 square kilometers), Bhutan is almost as big as Switzerland. Bhutan has a particularly close relationship with the Swiss Confederation and Austria, which are also mountainous countries.

339 EXCLUSIVE TRAVEL DESTINATION

Bhutan. Travel guides and many travel reports claim that Bhutan restricts the annual number of tourists to five thousand in order to preserve the uniqueness of the country. But, as recent visitor numbers show, this is not the case. Visitors to the country have now reached the five-figure range. However, the number of hotel beds and seats on airplanes may restrict wanderlust— plus the fact that every tourist must convert $240 into the local currency, the ngultrum, each day.

340 RACY PAINTINGS ON FAÇADES

Bhutan. Much to the delight of camera-wielding tourists, houses that are unmistakably decorated with drawings of phalluses are no rarity in the country. This art form originates from the Buddhist Chimi Lhakhang monastery, close to the former capital of Punakha, and it is a symbol of fertility and loosely defined happiness. Furthermore, these penises are said to protect against evil spirits and malicious gossip.

341 MUSEUM OF SOUVENIRS

Bandar Seri Begawan. What do you give to a ruler who is fabulously rich and already has everything? The sultanate of Brunei, a small country with vast oil and gas fields on the island of Borneo, answers this question in its Royal Regalia Museum in its capital, Bandar Seri Begawan. It displays regalia as well as gifts from state visitors. The rule for mosques also applies in the museum: please remove your shoes.

342 WORLD'S BIGGEST SETTLEMENT ON STILTS

Kampong Ayer. The sultan of Brunei donates much of his oil wealth to provide free schools and a healthcare system. He also provides aid for housing construction. Nevertheless, approximately twenty thousand citizens of Brunei choose to live in the historic settlement of Kampong, the largest stilt village settlement in the world. The buildings have now become one of the capital's tourist attractions, with a visitor center that demonstrates old crafts.

343 WHICH CAR SHOULD WE TAKE TODAY?

Brunei. Many news outlets are full of stories about the wealth of the sultan, whose family has ruled Bhutan for over six hundred years. Is it all true? Most of it certainly is, but all of it? The ruler allegedly owns around five thousand cars, including more than five hundred Mercedes, 180 BMWs, and 160 Porches. There are even a couple of Volkswagen cars in the royal garage, alongside 360 Bentleys and twenty Lamborghinis.

344 NO HIGHER THAN THE MINARET

Bandar Seri Begawan. The Omar Ali Saifuddien Mosque in Bandar Seri Begawan is located virtually in the center of the country, which is divided into two regions. The royal barge, which was rebuilt in stone (sixteenth century) in front of the mosque, is also one of the country's landmarks. The minaret is 144 feet (44 meters) high, and no building may be any taller. The national bank, which wanted to go higher, had to remove the top floor.

345 DON'T SLIP UP

Brunei is one of the strictest Muslim states in Asia, and the sale of alcohol is prohibited. However, non-Muslim tourists may import around two 2 liters for their own consumption, but they may not drink it in public and only discreetly sip on it in restaurants. Another potential slip-up, although not illegal: when greeting someone in the sultanate, men only shake men's hands, and women only shake women's hands.

346 A MATTER OF TIME

China. How many time zones are there in China, one of the four biggest countries in the world (along with Russia, Canada, and the US)? Just one: China Standard Time. The People's Republic, which was established after the Chinese civil war, abolished the previous five time zones. For comparison's sake: the US, which is about the same size, has five time zones, plus Hawaii time.

347 EUNUCHS FIT FOR A MUSEUM

Beijing. Close to Beijing, a eunuch museum remembers the men who had their penises and testicles removed as boys in order to serve at the imperial court and not run the risk of "pleasuring" the emperor's mistresses. The museum is close to the grave of the once-powerful eunuch named Tian Yi, whose grave gifts are missing. They include the bag in which he, like all other eunuchs, carried his genitals with him so that he could be a "man" again after his death.

348 CHINESE MARRIAGE MARKET

Shanghai. Internet dating? Speed dating? In China, marriage brokering is often done in the traditional way: parents seek out suitable marriage candidates for their children, even in a seemingly high-tech metropolis such as Shanghai. The process can be observed on Sundays in the public gardens, where parents advertise their son or daughter with a photo. If the child owns their own apartment, then they are favorites on the marriage market.

349 PAJAMAS OR NATIONAL DRESS

Shanghai. Before the world exhibition in Shanghai, the authorities tried, with moderate success, to put people off wearing pajamas in the streets by calling it "uncivilized." The organizers were right that tourists are snap happy when they see people dressed like that. The problem is most of the tourists think that it is national dress. Yet, this "fashion" began only relatively recently.

350 DON'T SLIP UP

The numerous cultural differences between China and the West become apparent in the case of table manners. In China it is permitted to eat noisily, to slurp, and to bring your dish up to your face in order to push food into your mouth with chopsticks. Burping is absolutely fine, and loud passing of gas is no rarity. Surprisingly, there are also some taboos. Don't blow your nose at the table (go to the restroom to do so). Also, don't eat everything on your plate; if you do, your host feels obliged to refill or reorder.

351 IF THE PRESSURE DROPS . . .

Qinghai / Lhasa. The "Tibet Train" might be the only train in the world that has a doctor on board and oxygen masks for every passenger, like in an airplane. The 1,215-mile (1,956 kilometer) stretch from Qinghai to the capital of Tibet, Lhasa, stops along the way at the highest train station in the world in Tanggula, which is 16,627 feet (5,068 meters) above sea level. From Lhasa on the "roof of the world," the tracks are to be extended to Nepal and India.

352 BE PREPARED WITH A YAK

Tibet. There are yaks everywhere in Tibet. The gregarious animals, which were domesticated by Tibetans, serve as beasts of burden—even on 16,404-foot-long (5,000 meter) mountain passes—and as a source of meat and leather, while their wool is used for clothing and tent canvas. Yaks' milk is made into cheese and butter, which is the basis for butter tea. The females of the species are called *dri*.

353 THE STORY OF THE GOLDEN TOILET

Hong Kong. In Hong Kong, the 3-D Goldshop has installed a toilet made of gold, which is worth more than $3 million. According to the owner, it was inspired by an anti-capitalist quote from Lenin. The toilet may be used only by customers who make purchases of at least $200. Taking a quick peek is cheaper. Apparently, a deceased billionaire already owned a golden toilet in Hong Kong.

354 LAST PLACE OF REST: THE INTERNET

Hong Kong. Over eight thousand high-rise buildings adorn the skyline of Hong Kong—a world record. The fact that there is not much ground space in the former British colony is also reflected in the cemeteries—or lack of them. Burial plots are very rare and correspondingly expensive: a plot in the Chinese Christian cemetery would cost around $15,000, if it were even available in the first place. So it's no surprise that in Hong Kong many mourners use virtual cemeteries.

355 WINNING BIG

Macau. The former Portuguese colony, a special administrative region of China, is the only place in China where gambling is permitted. And it is also successful; the city on the Pearl River even overtook Las Vegas in gambling revenues in 2006. In 2019, the takings at Macau's casinos amounted to more than $30 billion for the year, which was around five times more than the Las Vegas strip. (The biggest investors in Macau are US casinos.)

356 TOMB WITH A CORRECT BREAKING POINT

Agra. The Taj Mahal, the symbol of India, is the tomb that the Mughal emperor Shah Jahan commissioned to be built for his beloved third wife Mumtaz Mahal. Twenty-two thousand laborers are said to have worked on it for twenty-two years. The four minarets made of white marble appear to be as straight as pokers; however, they lean slightly outward. It is to prevent them from collapsing on the expensive mausoleum and damaging or destroying it in the event of an earthquake.

357 SMALLER LION'S SHARE

Gujarat. Of course, there are tigers in India, but lions? Yes, they also live on the subcontinent, albeit only on a reserve. The Asian lions are much smaller than their African cousins. At the start of the twentieth century, there were only a few left in Gir Forest in the Indian state of Gujarat, so the 545-square-mile (1,412 square kilometer) Gir National Park was established.

This coffee has already been digested before being served (no. 362).

358 ORDERED DUCK BUT GOT FISH

Mumbai. In the Indian metropolis of Mumbai, there is a dish called Bombay Duck on the menu—a name that sounds similar to Peking Duck. But if you order it and are looking forward to some fowl, you will be disappointed, because you will be served a dried and salt-cured lizard fish that has been caught in the Indian Ocean.

359 BUDDHA AND THE BODHI TREE

Bodh Gaya. Of the many Buddhist places of pilgrimage, the Bodhi Tree in Bodh Gaya (state of Bihar) is the most well known. It is said to have grown from an offshoot of the fig tree under which Buddha meditated. Today the temple is surrounded both by temples and souvenir shops, but the most desired souvenir is free: a leaf from the Bodhi Tree. However, they may not be picked; you may collect leaves only from the ground.

360 DON'T SLIP UP

Be it for business or for pleasure, in India you should always refuse the first invitation to a drink; otherwise, you will be thought of as greedy. People always ask a second time. Take your time in India; Western time constraints and appointments are not binding for Indians. Aficionados of the subcontinent ascribe this behavior to Hinduism. The religion, which originates in India, teaches a cycle of death and rebirth. In this philosophy, time is less important.

361 JOB TITLE: PASSENGER

Jakarta. Only private cars carrying at least three passengers are allowed to enter the Indonesian capital during the morning and evening rush hours. The government is trying to use this regulation to combat huge traffic jams. Many Indonesians get around this difficult-to-enforce provision by "renting" passengers, which provides additional income for the poor.

362 COFFEE FROM CATS

Indonesia. Indonesia produces the most expensive drink in the world: *kopi luwak*. This coffee has been sold for around $1,000 per pound on account of the coffee beans having journeyed through the digestive system of the palm civet native to Southeast Asia. The cat eats the coffee beans, which are then fermented. Because many civets are now kept in cages, the coffee prices are tending to fall.

363 WHEN BALI CLOSES DOWN

Bali. The island of Bali and other Hindu centers in Indonesia generally celebrate Nyepi, the new year, in March. It is a day of silence when public life closes down. There is no light or fires, and nobody may leave their homes—and that goes for tourists in hotels too. In the days before, there is ritual cleansing, and demons are banished using large dolls.

364 10-FOOT-LONG DRAGONS

Komodo. For a long time, researchers wondered how the "last dragon," the Komodo dragon, which can grow up to approximately 10 feet (3 meters) in length, caught its prey on Komodo and its neighboring islands. They believed it had poisonous saliva. It was only in 2009 that an Australian biologist discovered poison glands between the predator's teeth. The Komodo dragons normally eat only once per month, but they take on food equaling up to 80 percent of their body weight (150 pounds).

365 DON'T SLIP UP

If you go on vacation to Bali, you will likely visit a temple. To do so, everyone—including men and tourists—must wear a sarong, a knee-length cloth tied at the waist. You can often borrow the sarongs from the temple, but it is also worth buying one from a market stall, since they are practical on the beach and are a nice souvenir. Never climb any walls in a temple, even to frame the perfect photo. It is also strictly forbidden for women to visit a temple while menstruating.

366 SCREAMING IN THE SHRINE

Tokyo. Each year in April, the Senso-ji shrine in Tokyo plays host to a baby crying contest (*nakizumo*). Two young sumo wrestlers each hold a festively dressed small child, and a Shinto priest makes them cry by making faces at them. The first one to cry is the winner. This ceremony, which is also popular at other shrines, is said to improve the children's health.

367 MAN, OH MAN!

Kawasaki. Kanamara Matsuri is the festival of the steel penis that the megapolis of Kawasaki celebrates each year in April by holding a parade where participants carry giant penises to a shrine. Formerly, prostitutes prayed for health there, but today it is generally couples who pray for fertility, easy births, and good marriages. Penis-shaped sweets and cut vegetables are popular.

368 FOOTBATH IN THE TRAIN

Japan. On the Shinkansen Toreiyu bullet train, the JR East railway company offers a wagon with two footbaths that are 7 feet, 10 inches (2.4 meters) long. The passengers sit along the side of the bath, while the landscape rushes past the panorama windows. The elegant train was designed by Ken Okuyama, who also works for Ferrari cars.

369 LABYRINTH TOKYO

Tokyo. If you are looking for an address in Tokyo's sea of houses, you may despair. The houses on the street are not numbered as normal but are based on the order in which the planning permissions for the houses were approved. Only the most important streets have names. In emergencies, the numerous local police stations can help.

Before the New Year's celebrations on Bali, ritual cleansing is performed. Unlike in the Western world, Nyepi (new year) is a day of silence (no. 363).

This little squaller has a good chance of winning the baby crying contest in Tokyo (no. 366).

370 DON'T SLIP UP

Irasshaimase ("welcome") constantly echoes around every shop in Japan. In large stores, there are even young women standing at the doors to greet customers. However, if you actually answer these polite words, it confuses the shop employees. A friendly but silent smile is the suitable response.

371 THE FLAG WITH A TEMPLE

Cambodia. The Cambodian national flag is the only flag in the world with a building on it. It depicts a stylized image of the temple of Angkor Wat on a central red horizontal stripe with blue above and below it. The twelfth-century temple lost importance over the years, until it was researched in the nineteenth century. Today, Angkor Wat is Cambodia's main tourist attraction.

372 SPIDER ON RICE

Cambodia. Tarantulas—the large, hairy, and generally only slightly venomous spiders—are culinary delicacies for Cambodians. And it would not be a Cambodian meal if they weren't accompanied by the ever-present side dish: rice. So many meals are prepared with rice in Cambodia that it is not surprising that the word "rice" means the same as "food" in the Khmer language. These rice dishes include noodles and desserts with fruit and coconut milk.

373 THE LIPSTICK COCKTAIL

Phnom Penh. The city has a signature drink that was created in 1967, when Jackie Kennedy visited the Elephant Bar at the Hotel le Royal. The "femme fatale" is mixed from champagne, cognac, and crème de fraise, and then the glass is decorated with an orchid flower. The hotel saved Jackie's glass with her lipstick marks, although it does admit that it has since retouched her lipstick.

374 THE LONGEST ABC'S IN THE WORLD

Cambodia. Young students have it hard in Cambodia. They must learn the Khmer alphabet, with its seventy-one letters, not including some intermediate characters that are used to "Khmerise" Western words. The longest alphabet in the world originated in the sixth century and can be traced back to Indian scripts. It is perhaps a reason that Cambodia has a literacy rate of just 70 percent.

375 SPORTS FESTIVAL FOR THE DEAD

Cambodia. The Festival of the Dead, one of the most important celebrations in Cambodia, is not at all morbid. It is dedicated to ancestor worship. Over fifteen days in October, the ancestors whose spirits come to visit are offered food. The final day is devoted to entertaining them with traditional sports competitions, such as Khmer wrestling and other ancient martial arts such as *bokator* and *pradal serey*, in addition to horse and water buffalo racing.

376 TEST DRIVING A COFFIN

Seoul. Happy Dying is the name of Kim Giho's business in Seoul. She runs seminars in which people can prepare for their—hopefully distant—demise using role playing and PowerPoint presentations. The finale is lying in the coffin as the nails are hammered in but with the promise of "coming back to life" thirty minutes later.

377 A FUN PARK FOR ADULTS

Jeju. After going through the entrance shaped like a giant vulva, visitors to Love Land on the island of Jeju can expect to see a statue of a threesome that would demand gymnastic ability to re-create in real life. The 140 statues in the theme park on the honeymoon island show all imaginable positions of human copulation. There are even erect penises sticking out of the goldfish pond.

378 QUICK TRIP TO THE DEATH ZONE

Panmunjom. There is one tourist attraction for which you must sign a declaration that you are aware of the mortal danger before you visit: Panmunjom is in the demilitarized zone on the border with North Korea. Tourists can visit one of the huts on the border, as well as a North Korean tunnel, in addition to buying North Korean spirits.

379 UNIQUE TOILET

Suwon. There are plenty of toilet museums in Europe, Asia, and America. Many of them inform us that only a seventh of the world's population has access to a toilet. However, the toilet collection in Suwon in South Korea is unique because the building's architecture resembles a toilet bowl. In Korean the museum is called *haewoojae*, which means "worry-free refuge."

380 DON'T SLIP UP

Gestures in Asia often mean something different than they do in the West. Some of the body language that we use could be insulting in the Far East. For example, in Korea, don't wave at somebody with your palm facing upward because it is considered rude. It is particularly impolite to attract someone's attention with just one finger, because that is how you call dogs. If you want to politely attract someone's attention, turn your palm downward and waggle your fingers.

381 SPOILED WITH CHOICES

Malaysia. The country is an elected monarchy, which elects the predominantly ceremonial king from the ranks of the sultans every five years. In the country, the monarch holds the title *Kebawah Duli Yang Maha Mulia Seri Paduka Baginda Yang di-Pertuan Agong*—in short: *Yang di-Pertuan Agong*. (The emirs of the United Arab Emirates also elect a ruler, but they call him "president." The pope is an elected monarch who actually rules.)

382 STINKING MONSTER FLOWER

Borneo. The largest flower in the world grows on the island, which is divided among Malaysia, Indonesia, and Brunei. The rafflesia flower can reach up to approximately 3 feet (1 meter) in diameter and stinks dreadfully. Malaysia runs a conservation program for the approximately twenty types of rafflesia plant, which live on other plants as a parasite.

383 THE BIGGEST LEAVES IN THE WORLD

Borneo. Plants with huge leaves also grow in the Malaysian province of Sabah on Borneo. That is where the world's biggest solid leaf was discovered on an *Alocasia macrorrhiza* (the giant taro from the arum family). It measured 9 feet, 11 inches (3.02 meters) high and 6 feet, 4 inches (1.92 meters) wide. The largest split leaves in the world of flora are the approximately 66-foot-long (20 meter) palm fronds on the raffia palm.

384 THE RUBBER METROPOLIS

Kuala Kangsar. An offshoot from a "Ridley rubber tree" grows here. British biologist Henry Ridley smuggled seeds from Brazil that grew to make Malaysia a rubber world power. Today, palm oil is the main crop.

385 DON'T SLIP UP ———————— ————————

If you visit the Malayan state of Kelantan, which has long been ruled by the Islamic party, you should expect increasing levels of segregation according to sex. Men and women may not sit on the same park bench, and cinemas have had to close because it became law to have separate seats and lighting. Men and women have to join different lines at the supermarket. Women who wear a lot of makeup or dress flamboyantly must reckon with punishment.

386 UNDERWATER GOVERNMENT

Maldives. In 2009, the government of the Maldives took drastic action to make people aware of the biggest threat to their country: almost 1,200 islands being submerged in the Indian Ocean as a result of climate change and rising sea levels. The president and ministers met in diving gear for an underwater cabinet meeting, images of which went around the world. The atolls of the Maldives are just approximately 3 feet (1 meter) above sea level.

387 THE WORD HEARD AROUND THE WORLD

Maldives. The national language of the Maldives, Dhivehi, has contributed only one word to the international vocabulary of the world: *atholhu*, the atoll. Dhivehi is a language that arose from the Sinhalese language of the Middle Ages but has developed independently on the islands, which lie a good 620 miles (1,000 kilometers) southwest of Sri Lanka. In the national language, the country's name is Dhivehi Raajjeyge Jumhuriya ("Republic of Maldives").

388 ELECTORAL FRAUD WITH COCONUTS

Maldives. The Maldives is a devout Muslim country. However, the traditional belief in spirits is still very prevalent. A coconut that was found in a polling station during the 2013 elections was suspected of being connected with attempted election fraud—as everyone knows, coconuts often have spells placed on them.

389 AN ISLAND OF WASTE

Maldives. With 350,000 inhabitants and twice as many tourists, where is all the garbage that they produce going to go? The Maldives did not want to sacrifice a small island for this purpose, so they created one: Thilafushi. Land reclamation but with rubbish—at first glance, it looked like a success because it created space for industry and employment. However, Maldivian environmentalists are warning of toxic poisons in the waste, and the BBC in Great Britain called it "apocalyptic."

390 DON'T SLIP UP

Although the Maldivians separate the islands for locals from tourist islands, visitors may still not do everything. For example, going topless is strictly prohibited. Although the resorts are excepted from the general prohibition of alcohol, you may not bring your own alcohol into the country. Also, pork products will be confiscated on arrival and officially destroyed for being un-Islamic. Many Maldivians doubt whether that is also the case for the confiscated alcohol.

391 GENGHIS KHAN IS A HIT!

Mongolia. The country, which is one of the most sparsely populated in the world, was once ruled by military leaders Genghis Khan and Kublai Khan and was the center of a global empire. Today, Genghis Khan is omnipresent; the airport in the capital Ulaanbaatar is named in his honor, and approximately 34 miles (55 kilometers) out of town, he rises out of the steppe, sitting on the biggest equestrian statue in the world.

392 EGG HUNT WITH "INDIANA JONES"

Gobi. American scientist and adventurer Roy Chapman Andrews (1884–1960) explored the Gobi Desert and was the first researcher to discover dinosaur eggs. And, as a crack shot, he also knew how to defend himself against Mongolian robbers. He later became the director of the American Museum of Natural History and was famous for his dangerous missions. He is considered to be the inspiration for Hollywood's "Indiana Jones."

393 AND THE MONEY STINKS!

Mongolia. The Mongolian currency, called Tögrög or Tugrik, shows a portrait of Genghis Khan, as is to be expected. It is issued in large bills for convenience; for example, an overnight stay in a tourist hotel in Ulaanbaatar costs 40,000 Tögrög. In the country of shepherds and sheep, it is said that the bills, which are now minted in Great Britain, smell unmistakably of sheep after just a short time in circulation.

394 A TENT FOR THE WORLD

Mongolia. The yurt, the large tent of Mongolian nomads (called *ger* in Mongolian), is embarking on an international career. On many camping sites, the stable wooden structures are enjoyed as an alternative to log cabins. Luxury yurts are particularly popular for so-called glamping. Also gaining global popularity are "Mongolian barbecues"; they, however, have nothing to do with Mongolia and hail from Taiwan.

395 CHARITABLE CAR RACE

England / Ulan Ude. The Mongol Rally is an absurd car race, which starts in England and originally ended in Ulaanbaatar. It does not have a winner, and there are only three rules: (1) your car engine must be 1 liter or less, (2) you are on your own, and (3) each team must raise 1,000 British pounds for charity. For tax reasons, the journey now ends in Ulan Ude in Russia.

396 THIS BARK PROTECTS AGAINST (ALMOST) EVERYTHING

Myanmar (Burma). Again and again, you meet women, men, and children in Myanmar (Burma) who have more or less artfully drawn on their faces with a whitish-yellow paste. *Thanaka* is a traditional natural cosmetic that is made from the grated bark of the crab apple tree. It protects and cools the skin against the sun, and it is also said to smooth wrinkles and help against colds.

397 EVERYTHING HANGING BY A HAIR

Kyaikto. The golden rock on Mount Kyaiktiyo is a pilgrimage site that only a handful of foreign tourists get to see, despite attracting thousands of locals each year. According to the legend, the granite stone, which is completely gold-plated, is prevented from falling into the abyss by a strand of Buddha's hair. Women are permitted to touch only a smaller replica that is also gold-plated.

398 ARTISTIC BALL BALANCING

Myanmar (Burma). The Burmese have a sport in which the winners are those who give the best dance performance. To play *chinlone*, a 1,500-year-old game, five players move in a circle. They and a "dancing" soloist in the center attempt to keep the cane ball in the air for as long as possible. They may use their feet and knees but not their hands.

399 MYANMAR'S BEST GRAPES

Taunggyi. Myanmar (Burma) is not a name on the lips of wine experts. However, a German from Düsseldorf wants to change that. With his partners, Bert Morsbach has established Aythaya Vineyard on the hilly slopes of Shan State as Burma's first vineyard. With ten thousand vine stocks from Europe, he produces 100,000 bottles of shiraz, sauvignon blanc, and other wines per year. A restaurant and a bungalow complex complete the exotic attraction.

400 DON'T SLIP UP

In Myanmar, tourists like to wear the national dress: the *longyi*. It is a wraparound skirt made of a long piece of cloth. The locals often chuckle when they see male tourists wearing them like women and female tourists wearing them like men. The men's *paso* is tied in front of the stomach, while the women's *htamein* is tied to the side at the hip. Another tip: if you hear kissing-like sounds in a restaurant, you should not suspect any romancing—it is how to attract the waiters' attention.

401 PERMANENT TEMPORARY SOLUTION ON EVEREST

Mount Everest. At 29,032 feet (8,849 meters), Mount Everest is the biggest mountain in the world and the pride of Nepal, although it is also shared with China. It was named for Sir George Everest (1790–1866), the surveyor general of what was then known as British India. He actually never surveyed this mountain. His successor in India, Andrew Waugh, had originally intended it to be a temporary name. Incidentally, Everest pronounced his name "Ivrist."

402 DEEP LAKE IN THE HIGHLANDS

Mount Everest. Mount Everest, currently 29,032 feet high, is still growing—albeit just a few millimeters per year. With it, the "Yellow Band" is also getting higher. At about 1,968 to 3,937 feet (600 to 1,200 meters) under the summit, it runs through the rocks and consists of maritime limestone. It is a leftover from Tethys Ocean on the Indian Plate, which shifted north and collided with the European Plate to create the Himalayas.

403 POINTED FLAG

Nepal. At the flag parade outside the headquarters of the United Nations in New York, the flag of Nepal is particularly noticeable. It is the only flag that is not rectangular but instead consists of two triangles placed over each other. The upper triangle shows the moon and the lower one shows the sun. They are symbols of Hinduism and Buddhism, both of which have shaped the country. The points represent the Himalayas, and the design is over two thousand years old.

404 THE TEACHER IS NEVER RIGHT

Nepal. The only living goddesses in the world reside in temples in Nepal. The *kumaris* (girls/virgins) are selected as small children from among the Buddhist elite and are honored in religious festivals. When they reach puberty, they return to normal life. Previously, they were regarded as omniscient, but now they are given private lessons—a difficult task for their tutor, since nobody may contradict a goddess.

405 LITTLE MONSTER MACHINES

Nepal. Yeti Airlines is the biggest domestic Nepalese airline. It visually honors its namesake, the mythical Himalayan monster, on the fins of its airplanes with a larger-than-life footprint, the logo of the airline established in 1998. Its subsidiary, Tara, flies seven smaller machines, including two Dornier Do 228 aircraft, which can also take off and land on short runways.

406 THE NEVER-ENDING CONSTRUCTION

Pyongyang. In 1987, work began on the "tallest building in the world," the substantial 105-floor Ryugyong Hotel in Pyongyang, the capital of North Korea. The three-thousand-room hostel shaped like a paper rocket has not opened to date. At 1,082 feet (330 meters) tall, it is still only the thirty-fifth tallest building in the world. *Esquire* magazine called it "the worst building in the history of mankind."

407 MOTHER'S DAY AT CHRISTMAS

North Korea. Christmas in North Korea? Nope! The state does not permit any Christian celebrations. Instead, on December 24, Kim Jong-suk is honored. She died in 1949 and was the mother of the "Dear Leader" Kim Jong-il (who died in 2011). Valentine's Day? Of course not! That also does not exist in North Korea. Instead, the country celebrates the birthday of Kim Jong-il on February 16.

408 LEGENDARY GREEN

Pyongyang. Golf in North Korea? It is at least theoretically possible if you can get your hands on a rare tourist visa, but it appears that the only golfing green in the country is usually reserved for bigwigs in the government. However, if you make it onto the eighteen-hole course, you will be golfing on historic ground: Kim Jong-il is reported to have sunk a hole-in-one during his first-ever round of golf there.

409 HAIRCUT CATALOG

Pyongyang. The barbers of Pyongyang have difficulty expressing their artistic side, because their customers may choose among only twenty-eight permitted hairstyles, of which women have the greater selection. The rules for men dictate that no hair may extend longer than 2 inches from the skin. However, the proclamation that all Koreans must have the same haircut as the president is an internet joke.

410 DON'T SLIP UP

The list of restrictions is long in the totalitarian country of North Korea. Things such as binoculars or radios are prohibited, and conversations about politics and the adoration of the three Kim presidents are unwelcome. In the Kumsusan mausoleum, men are expected to wear ties, and you should bow in front of important monuments. Tips are not the norm; only your own tourist guide and tourist bus driver would expect about $5 per day.

411 A TENT AS A MOSQUE

Islamabad. The symbol of the city, the Shah Faisal Mosque offers space for seventy thousand believers and is one of the largest Islamic places of worship in the world. The building, which was modeled on a Bedouin tent, was funded by Saudi Arabia and named for its king. The globe of lights inside was designed by German Johannes Dinnebier.

412 THE HIGHEST PAVED ROAD IN THE WORLD

Pakistan / China. The highest international paved road in the world, the Karakoram Highway, has linked Pakistan to China since 1986. The road, which is just under 8,077 miles (1,300 kilometers) long, runs over the 15,220-foot-high (4,693 meter) Khunjerab pass in the Karakoram mountain range. China is currently widening the highway to several lanes in order to be able to ship more wares from Pakistani ports and to support tourism along the Silk Road.

413 NEW VALLEY IN OLD MOUNTAINS

Hunza Valley. The Hunza Valley, previously accessible only by foot via dangerous tracks, was made accessible through the construction of the Karakoram Highway. The former princely state is approximately 8,200 feet (2,500 meters) above sea level and has become a tourist destination due to its spectacular mountain scenery, in particular the scenery around Fort Baltit. Now, Hunza cuisine has been discovered, which among other things is famous for *maltash*, an aged butter.

414 GAME WITHOUT RULES

Gilgit. Shandur Top in the Pakistani province of Gilgit is home to the highest polo field in the world. Local polo teams have been meeting on the field at 12,139 feet (3,700 meters) above sea level since 1936 for a tournament that even attracts visitors from abroad. The reason: below the Shandur Pass, "traditional polo" is played, with six players and horses per team. There's only one rule: there are no rules! Nor are there any umpires.

415 TURNING HEXAGONS INTO BALLS

Sialkot. A suitable souvenir from Pakistan? A soccer ball! The field-hockey-and-cricket-mad nation is the world's biggest producer of handsewn soccer balls. The epicenter of the ball production is the tradition-steeped industrial town of Sialkot. Forty to sixty million soccer balls are sewn together each year, mainly in small businesses. In World Cup years, that could amount to 70 percent of the world production.

416 ONE FLAG TWO WAYS

Philippines. The flag of the Philippines has a special feature. Normally, it has one blue (upper) band and one red (lower) band, with a white triangle showing the sun and three stars. These triangles extend from the flagpole into the colored bands. However, in times of war, the red band is on top and the blue one is below. The flag was designed in 1879 by Emilio Aguinaldo, a revolutionary leader who went on to become president. The colors are said to be reminiscent of Cuba or the USA.

417 I WISH IT COULD BE CHRISTMAS EVERY DAY

Philippines. If you get annoyed at the end of August because of Christmas chocolate in the supermarket, then you should avoid traveling to the Philippines. Their yuletide with all the Santa decorations and "Jingle Bells"-style music lasts from September until Epiphany. And if you can endure "Simbang Gabi" and attend all nine masses in the nights before Christmas Eve, your wishes will come true.

418 DRASTIC EASTER RITUAL

Philippines. During Holy Week before Easter, some Filipino believers also celebrate a little differently. During Penitensya, men flog their backs on the way to the hill of crosses, and others let themselves be nailed to crosses—all voluntarily. The government likes the religious spectacle because it attracts increasing numbers of tourists.

419 VOLCANIC EASTER

Camiguin. The island in the southern Philippines covers only 89 square miles (230 square kilometers) but has seven volcanoes. That is the world record for the most volcanoes per square mile. After the eruption of Mount Vulcan in 1871, a way of the cross was created with fourteen stations that lead up the mountain. It marks the end of the Easter procession, which is approximately 40 miles (64 kilometers) long and circles the island.

420 DON'T SLIP UP

Even for official occasions, Filipino men often wear a *barong tagalog*, shortened to *baro*. The lightweight, loose-fitting, and transparent shirt is worn over a simple white shirt and is never tucked into the trousers—very comfortable in tropical temperatures. For celebrations, many men wear *baros* that are embroidered on the front. A normal shirt is not suitable as a *baro*. Now and again, women wear elegant *barong tagalogs*.

421 BEST STAY CLEAN!

Singapore. The city-state of Singapore is most likely the cleanest city in the world, and if you break the rules, you can reckon with harsh punishment. Not flushing in a public restroom results in a five-hundred-dollar fine. It costs ten times as much to relieve yourself in an elevator. The locals speak of a *fine city*, referring both to the beauty and penalties.

422 SONGBIRD CONTEST

Singapore. Every morning, but especially on Sundays, many bird enthusiasts gather with their singing feathered friends in the Ang Mo Kio public gardens. The birds put on a free concert while their owners debate whether a *mata puteh* (an Indian white eye) or *merbok* (a zebra dove) has the better song. The response comes without hesitation from the cages, some of which have been beautifully carved.

423 CONCRETE JUNGLE TREES

Singapore. Already a green city, Singapore has established a 133.4-acre (54 hectare) park with two greenhouses on newly reclaimed land. The biggest attraction is the 59-to-164-foot-tall (18 to 50 meter) "supertrees," which are made from concrete and steel. These "trees" are ventilation shafts, and some of them have solar panels to generate energy. The two largest ones are connected by a bridge that doubles as a viewing platform.

424 NOBODY KNOWS THE RECIPE

Singapore. The Singapore Sling was created in 1915 in Raffles Hotel. The original recipe of the cocktail is unknown, but a drink consisting of gin, cherry brandy, Bénédictine, and pineapple juice is served a thousand times per evening in the Long Bar at Raffles. While today's bar is not the birthplace of the drink, the establishment is unique nevertheless: elsewhere in Singapore, dirtiness is punished, but here you can throw peanut shells on the floor.

425 CHRISTMASTIME

Singapore. A little bit of imagination and some large dollar bills make it snow in Singapore for the holidays. Every year, the Christmas Garden in Tanglin Mall, not far from Orchard Road, attracts families from mid-November onward. Twice each evening, snow cannons shower artificial snow; there is also a foam avalanche for children.

426 ADAM'S LANDING PLACE

Adam's Peak. Adam's Bridge, also known in old documents as Rama's Bridge, is an approximately 19-mile-long (30 kilometer) chain of small islands and sandbanks in the strait between southern India and the northern tip of Sri Lanka. According to Muslim and Christian legend, Adam fell out of heaven over Sri Lanka and landed on Adam's Peak, which is 7,359 feet (2,243 meters) above sea level. He then crossed over the "bridge" to get to India.

427 CAPITAL CONFUSION

Kotte. What is the capital of Sri Lanka, the country formerly known as Ceylon? This makes for a tricky trivia question, because many would assume it is Colombo. However, in 1982 the parliament and the political elite moved to Sri Jayawardenepura Kotte, a suburb of Colombo, which is normally simply called Kotte after a fortress ("Kotte") from the thirteenth century. It later gained the honorary title Sri Jayawardenepura, meaning "the blessed fortress city of growing victory."

428 A LITTLE TOUCH-UP

Sigiriya. One of the most famous attractions in Sri Lanka is Sigiriya, an almost 656-foot-high (200 meter) rock, which was once home to a royal fortress. If you climb up the side steps, you will pass the "cloud maidens": twenty-two pretty frescos of young topless women. In the 1970s the pictures were restored, with a little "plastic surgery" too.

429 CITY OF LEATHER TROUSERS

Katunayake. Surprisingly, the majority of German "Bavarian" lederhosen (leather trousers) come from Sri Lanka. The factory in Katunayake also supplies trousers in the style of Steiermark and Salzkammergut, both in Austria. It is busy season before the Oktoberfest, although the seamstresses are employed throughout the whole year. They are reported to have giggled the first time they saw the trouser design with the large codpiece. Incidentally, the majority of leather shorts are made from goatskin.

430 DESIRED POWDER

Sri Lanka. "You can already smell the cinnamon when you are 45 kilometers [28 miles] off the coast," noted a Dutch captain in the seventeenth century. At that time, the country that is now Sri Lanka held a very profitable monopoly for the desired and expensive spice from the bark of the native cinnamon tree. In the olden days, it was a present for kings and an offering to the gods. The monopoly has long since collapsed, but cinnamon has become a popular souvenir from Sri Lanka.

431 BREAKFAST WITH THE ANCESTORS

Keelung. On the last two days of August each year, the Taiwanese celebrate the Ghost Festival, with the biggest one held in Keelung City. According to popular Asian belief, in the seventh month of the moon calendar, the ghosts of the ancestors come visiting. After a night full of events, at six o'clock an altar with breakfast is set up to bid farewell to the ghosts; after eleven o'clock the living may eat what remains.

432 A COFFEE IN THE CREMATORIUM

Taipei. At Funeral Parlour No. 2, a crematorium in Taiwanese capital Taipei, the bereaved take leave of their loved ones in a special way. During the approximately one-and-a-half-hour cremation, they can drink a coffee in the cafeteria. The coffee machine and the air-conditioning of the restaurant are powered by waste heat from the cremation furnace. The relatives can take the urn home with them afterward.

433 PARADISE À LA ARMY

Kinmen. The Taiwanese island of Kinmen, which lies just off mainland China, was heavily fought over between 1949 and 1958. Taiwan stationed up to 100,000 soldiers there. The army constructed a "special house" for them. It was a brothel, outside which the men queued with tickets. This "military paradise" is now a museum that tells the story of the brothel and the island.

434 PEARL TEA

Taiwan. In the 1980s, Taiwan made a contribution to the culinary culture of the world with the invention of bubble tea. The black tea or green tea, mixed with milk or fruit juice, has tapioca balls added to it. Later, these balls were replaced by algae products. Some variations include "pearls" that burst in your mouth. The sweet tea is still popular in Asia and around the world.

435 DON'T SLIP UP

In the Chinese cultural region, red is a symbol of good luck. But in Taiwan, red ink is taboo. It brings bad luck, so it is best not to use it. Many Taiwanese even avoid red pens. The superstition is based in reality: at one time the prisons wrote the names of the prisoners condemned to death in red ink.

436 168 LETTERS FOR BANGKOK

Bangkok. The ceremonial name of Bangkok is Krung Thep Mahanakhon Amon Rattanakosin Mahinthara Ayuthaya Mahadilok Phop Noppharat Ratchathani Burirom Udomratchaniwet Mahasathan Amon Piman Awatan Sathit Sakkathattiya Witsanukam Prasit. The name is generally shortened to Krung Thep. In 1989, the Thai rock group Asanee-Wasan made a song out of the long name. The name Bangkok is used only internationally.

437 HOLY BUDDHA

Bangkok. The Emerald Buddha, who sits in the temple named for him in Bangkok, is Thailand's patron saint. He is thought to have miraculous powers, such as the ability to bestow individual wealth or to ward off epidemics. However, despite the name, the statue is not made of emerald but was carved out of a large block of jade. He is called the "Emerald Buddha" only on account of his green color.

Stand back, train approaching! The sellers at this market are unfazed by it (no. 438).

438 A MARKET RUNNING ON SCHEDULE

Samut Songkhram. The "market of closing umbrellas" (*talad rom hub*) owes its name to the fact that it is done eight times a day. Upon a signal, all the market stands—with their canvas roofs and parasols—are pulled to the side. Then a train passes through the market, just inches from the stands and over the top of baskets of wares that fit precisely between the tracks.

439 A FEAST FOR THE MONKEYS

Lopburi. A monkey-like happiness settles over the city in November thanks to the Monkey Buffet Festival, which is organized by Lopburi Province and takes place outside the Phra Prang Sam Yot temple. A huge, mainly fruit buffet is prepared for around six hundred monkeys that live in the area. The inhabitants say that it is to thank the monkeys, who attract tourists to the region. The festival itself has also become a big attraction.

440 DON'T SLIP UP

Even though many tourists are unaware that Thailand is a monarchy, the king is greatly revered. Insulting him is a punishable offense. Hence, conversations about the monarchy are best avoided. Since all paper money shows a likeness of the king, you are committing an offense if you write on a bill. The same applies if, even accidentally, you stand on a bill lying on the floor.

441 THE FAMILY VEHICLE

Vietnam. This country is moped country. More than ten million motorcycles are on the road in the state of ninety million inhabitants. Therefore, there are nine Vietnamese per moped—and you often get the impression that it is not just a statistic. At least four people (father, mother, and two children) riding a bike at once is not uncommon. The constant stream of mopeds has become a tourist attraction.

442 THREE DAYS OF CELEBRATION

Vietnam. Tết Nguyên Đán, generally just called Tết, is Vietnam's lunar new year. The most important celebration in the country occurs between January 21 and February 21. Before the three-feast day, people traditionally pay off their debts (naturally not excluding government debt). Many families put up a "New Year tree," which is generally a long bamboo cane or a flowering branch decorated with origami.

443 CAVE WORLD RECORD

Phong Nha-Ke Bang National Park. In 2009, when experts in north Vietnam explored the Hang Son Doong Cave, which was discovered only in 1991, they were thrilled. It meant they were able to take the world record from the Deer Cave in Malaysia. Their mountain stream cave was much bigger—up to 656 feet (200 meters) high and 295 feet (90 meters) wide. It's so large that a New York City block with several forty-story skyscrapers could fit inside. There are two places where the roof has collapsed, and in these depths a jungle is growing.

444 SNAKE WINE AS A SOUVENIR

Vietnam. Who invented this? The Vietnamese. Who copied it? Half of Asia. The "snake wine": rice wine or spirit with a preserved venomous snake was once used only as medicine but has now become a top tourist souvenir—even though the bottles may not be brought into many countries. The story that a cobra survived three months in a bottle and then bit a woman is met with much skepticism.

445 DON'T SLIP UP

If you are invited to a Vietnamese home, you should know that it is generally only a polite gesture and you should excuse yourself with other duties. It is only the second invitation that is really meant. Furthermore, as a guest you should not stick chopsticks into the rice bowl, which is considered as a precursor to death, as is believed in many other "rice nations" as well. You may rest your chopsticks on the table; marks on the table are considered a sign of a good meal.

Christmas Island in the Indian Ocean is part of Australia and is famous for its crabs (no. 446).

OCEANIA

446 CHRISTMAS COMES TWICE HERE!

Kiribati. Navigators, watch out! Our planet has two Christmas Islands. Christmas Island in the Indian Ocean is part of Australia, while Christmas Island in the Pacific is part of the Republic of Kiribati, which is made up of one island and thirty-two coral atolls. Tired of all the confusion, Kiribati has renamed its island and it is now called Kiritimati, which means Christmas in the local language.

447 EASTWARD TO THE MILLENNIUM

Kiribati. The island state is the only country in the world to stretch over all four hemispheres. It is one of the biggest countries in the world yet has only 313 square miles (811 square kilometers) of land. However, its maritime territory covers a whopping 1 million square miles (3 million square kilometers). Kiribati celebrated a questionable premiere: it was the first country in the world to welcome the new millennium after having moved the international date line to its eastern boundaries in 1995.

448 EASTER TRADITIONS

Australia. Hares are rare but unpopular in Australia. They are confused with rabbits, which are hated Down Under due to their large numbers. So conservationists had the idea of replacing the Easter Bunny with a native animal: the bilby, which is threatened with extinction. The big-eared marsupial is related to kangaroos and koalas. You can buy chocolate bilbies around Easter time, and some of the profits go to conservation projects for the species. However, Australian consumers still favor the Easter Bunny over the Easter Bilby.

449 THE BIGGEST WAR MEMORIAL IN THE WORLD

Victoria. The splendid Great Ocean Road along the coastline southwest of Melbourne is more than just a tourist attraction in Australia. At a length of 151 miles (243 kilometers), it is also the biggest war memorial in the world and is dedicated to Australia's fallen soldiers from World War I. The famous road was hewn out of cliffs by returning soldiers, who were unemployed.

450 SPACE WASTE DISPOSAL

Western Australia. The demise of the first US space station was announced with the following message on Australian radio in 1979: "Skylab has safely entered the South Atlantic." A few seconds later, the 75-ton device shot over the town of Esperance and crashed a little farther southwest. Since then, parts of Skylab have been kept in the Museum of Esperance, and the municipality sent the US a four-hundred-Australian-dollar fine for "environmental pollution."

451 DON'T SLIP UP

The "Aussies" are generally relaxed and fun companions. And although it is true that the first white settlers were prisoners, jokes by foreign tourists about their not-so-illustrious ancestors annoy the Australians.

452 JOURNEY TO "MIDDLE EARTH"

Matamata. The Maori name for New Zealand is Aotearoa, which means "land of the long white cloud." Today, the country is more famous as Middle Earth from J. R. R. Tolkien's novels *The Lord of the Rings* and *The Hobbit*. Thanks to the popular films, New Zealand has generated millions in new tourist income, and the "Hobbiton" film sets in Matamata are one of the main attractions. Originally, they were intended to be dismantled after filming.

453 THE FIRST RAYS OF SUN

Gisborne. During the Southern Hemisphere summer, the first sunlight of the day can be seen from the summit of 2,444-foot-high (1,745 meter) Mount Hikurangi in New Zealand (at least if you discount New Zealand's remote Chatham Islands). Although Fiji and Tonga are closer to the international date line in the Pacific, the summer sun is first visible in New Zealand due to the angle of the Earth's axis.

454 THE CLEAREST WATER IN THE WORLD

Nelson Lakes National Park. The Blue Lake, with underwater visibility of 230 to 260 feet (70 to 80 meters), is the clearest lake in the world. The clarity is thanks to its location in the mountains at 3,940 feet (1,200 meters) above sea level, with few trees, and also because the running water is filtered through rock. Bathing or diving in the (very cold) lake is not permitted because the Indigenous people, the Maoris, consider it to be sacred.

455 EASTER TRADITIONS

New Zealand. There are always celebrations on the Tuesday after Easter in Taihape, New Zealand, the ironically self-proclaimed "Gumboot Capital of the World" in honor of the Wellington boot. The highlight of the celebrations is the welly-throwing contest. However, tourists can test out their waterproof boots any day. It is not clear if "Gumboot Day" will continue, because the local rubber boot factory has now closed—but the giant boot that greets visitors will remain.

456 A CHANGE FROM ROTTEN TOMATOES

Palmerston North. After a rather unsuccessful performance, British comedian John Cleese (of Monty Python) described the town as the suicide capital of New Zealand. He claimed that it's the place to be if you want to kill yourself. A few months later, the citizens of the town got their revenge and named their 138-foot-high (42 meter) trash dump "Mount Cleese." The sign bearing its name has become a favorite photo opportunity for tourists.

457 BISMARCKS, WHEREVER YOU LOOK

Papua New Guinea. The Bismarcks are a popular namesake in Papua New Guinea, which was once a German colony. The Bismarck Archipelago—named for Otto von Bismarck—counts two hundred islands and is located north of the main island. The largest mountain in the country, at 14,793 feet (4,509 meters), is Mount Wilhelm, named after Bismarck's son Wilhelm. And it is surrounded by his "family": Ottoberg (after Otto, a former German chancellor), as well as Marienberg and Herbertberg (after Otto's other children). The suffix "berg" means mountain in German.

458 SPEAKING GERMAN ON THE EQUATOR

Papua New Guinea. Papua New Guinea is the country with the most language diversity in the world. Its 7.3 million inhabitants speak 830 different languages. In order to be able to communicate, the colonial Tok Pisin (also known as New Guinean pidgin), a simple variation of English with a few German words, was developed. On the Bismarck Archipelago, the people even spoke "Unserdeutsch," the only pidgin language that has its roots in German.

459 SWINES FOR STATUS

Papua New Guinea. How many pigs does a wife cost? In Papua New Guinea, that is a matter for negotiation. The more a clan has invested in the training of their daughters, the more pigs are owed, with fifteen porkers as the minimum. The animals romp about the small towns in inland areas, because the number of pigs also indicates the social status of the residents. They are roasted only for special celebrations.

Boys wearing the traditional dress of the Trobriand Islands. White people are considered ugly here (no. 460).

460 NO SEX FOR TOURISTS

Trobriand Islands. *Bukumatula* huts, where teenagers can have their first sexual experiences, still exist in the villages on the Trobriand Islands. If babies are made in the process, then the children are brought up by the villagers. All attempts by missionaries to change this practice failed. However, in the era of AIDS, the authorities do encourage contraception. Incidentally, white people don't stand much chance with Trobriand locals, because they think pale skin is ugly.

461 TAKA TUKA LAND ON THE MAP

Tabar Island. As all *Pippi Longstocking* readers know, Ephraim Longstocking is Pippi's father and king of the South Sea island Taka Tuka Land. Astrid Lindgren, the author, was inspired by Swedish sailor Carl Emil Pettersson, who washed up on Tabar Island in 1904 after a shipwreck. He married the local king's daughter, and after the death of his father-in-law, he became king himself.

462 WEIGH-IN AT CHECK-IN

Samoa. Obesity has become a major issue on many South Pacific islands. Among the countries with troubling statistics about obesity per capita is Samoa. Samoa Air calculates the price of airfares according to body weight and luggage.

463 ALWAYS A NEW DAY

Samoa. Originally Samoa sat east of the international date line, which runs through the center of the Pacific. It meant that Samoa was one of the first countries to welcome the new day. Since that situation was not practical for trade with the US, in 1892 Samoa changed its time to the "old day." Trade is currently flowing eastward, so in 2011 Samoa skipped December 30 and reverted back to the "new day."

464 HOME OF THE CREATOR OF *TREASURE ISLAND*

Apia. Samoa, just like the other South Sea islands, has beautiful countryside and beaches. However, the biggest attraction of the island state is a world-famous Scot who died there: Robert Louis Stevenson. The author of *Treasure Island* was given the honorary title of Tusitala ("teller of tales") by the Samoans. Today, Villa Vailima, his large house close to the capital city of Apia, is one of the most popular museums in Polynesia.

465 PYRAMIDS IN THE SOUTH SEAS

Savai'i. Admittedly, Samoa's "star pyramid" on the Samoan island of Savai'i does not match Egypt's offerings, neither in height (up to 39 feet) nor in age (constructed between 1000 and 1400 CE). Even the layout (197 feet by 231 feet) is comparatively small compared to the Egyptian giants. But the basalt pyramid, which is also known as Pulemelei Mound, is the biggest and oldest in Polynesia. The purpose of the pyramid is unknown.

466 "RAIN" FOR HOLLYWOOD

Pago Pago. The capital of American Samoa owes its "film career" to a visit by the author Somerset Maugham in the 1920s. After his stay, he set his short story "Rain" on the island. The story of a prostitute and a preacher became a success on stage and was filmed three times: once with Gloria Swanson (1928), then with Joan Crawford (1932), and finally with Rita Hayworth (1953). Hollywood, what about another remake?

467 WEALTH IN ROCKS

Yap. The island in the Federated States of Micronesia is always mentioned in the history of money because it has unique "coins." They are stone discs with a diameter ranging from 2.75 to 142 inches (7 to 360 centimeters). Their value is denoted not only in terms of their size but also according to the history of the stone, which after a change of ownership remains in the same place. Furthermore, the stone currency is used as a dowry or for other traditional purposes.

The inhabitants of Micronesia have a wealth of stones. These large stone discs are still used as "coins" (no. 467).

468 SLIGHTLY DIFFERENT TV FEES

Tuvalu. At the end of the 1980s, when the country domain name extensions for internet addresses were allocated, the island state of Tuvalu was given ".tv." Because the two letters are coveted in the entertainment world, the poor atoll country rented them out for twelve years at a cost of $50 million (US). Even the follow-up contracts bring in millions per year. Despite this lucrative business idea, the eleven thousand inhabitants of Tuvalu are reliant on international development aid.

469 MICKEY MOUSE MONEY

Niue. The island of Niue is also making money with the internet domain name extension ".nu." The buyers are primarily erotic-services providers in French-speaking countries, because *nu* means naked. It is therefore fitting that the coral island was the "first Wi-Fi nation in the world" providing free internet access. Niue has also tried to raise its profile and earn money by minting unusual coinage. For example, the coins depict Donald Duck or characters from *Star Wars* and *Dr. Who*.

470 FRUSTRATION WITHOUT FERTILIZATION

Nauru. Thanks to bird-dropping fertilizer, Nauru was still the richest country on Earth in 1968. However, now the guano supply has been exhausted, and the country is reliant on international aid. Since its airline went into liquidation, only a few tourists make their way to the island. Nevertheless, Nauru's flag provides a geography lesson to those who don't know where the island is. A band of gold separates the blue flag (above: the sky, and below: the Pacific), and a large white star shows the location of the island.

471 AN ISLAND RISING OUT OF THE SOUTH SEA

Tonga. The year 2019 saw it happen again: Tonga gained a new island. A submarine volcano created the new island, which is 1,312 feet (400 meters) long and 328 feet (100 meters) wide. At the same time, a young island close by disappeared. It is a continuous giving and taking in the South Seas' last monarchy. The number of islands is always just a snapshot of a given moment in time. Therefore, in official statistics, it says that there are "over 170 islands and atolls." Meanwhile, it continues to rumble deep below Tonga.

472 SELF-ADHESIVE BANANAS

Tonga. The stamps in the Kingdom of Tonga enjoy global popularity as a souvenir. Since the 1960s they have been "self-adhesive," an innovation that both Tonga and Sierra Leone (in West Africa) claim as their own. Tonga's stamps in the shape of a banana with a value of just one Seniti were a philatelic world sensation in 1969.

473 HIP MATS WITH ALL DUE RESPECT

Tonga. They are noticeable: the mats that many men and some women wrap around their hips. No Tongan would dare appear at an important occasion without a *ta'ovala*. It is a sign of respect both to the king and to their fellow citizens. Sometimes, you see very tattered mats (mainly made of pandanus). They are inherited mats that have been in the respective family for a long time.

474 NEVER ON A SUNDAY

Nuku'alofa. One minute past midnight on Mondays used to be a popular time to meet at the cinema because the strict Sunday rest was over. It is a custom that was and is still observed in Tonga more than any other Christian country. On Sundays, all commercial activities, as well as fishing and swimming, are prohibited. The few exceptions—for example, for a bakery or a hotel—must be officially approved.

475 DON'T SLIP UP

The Kingdom of Tonga is a conservative and religious country, so much so that it is frowned upon to show too much skin. Going topless is an absolute no-go, even for men. It is said that Tonga's police have punished male cruise tourists for this by putting them in the cells of Tonga's small capital, Nuku'alofa, until their ships were ready to depart. Men may wear shorts, but not on Sundays, and shorts should cover their knees where possible.

Pink flamingos as far as the eye can see in Lake Nakuru in Kenya. The birds' feathers get their color from the small crabs that the flamingos eat (no. 494).

AFRICA

476 TERRORIST ATTACK ON THE SPHINX

Giza. In 1378, the fanatic Muhammad Sa'im al-Dahr knocked the nose off the sphinx of Giza. Back then, an angry mob lynched him. But the question remains unanswered: What is the purpose of the sphinx?

477 DESECRATOR OF THE ROYAL MONUMENT

Giza. At the original entrance to the Great Pyramid of Giza, you will find engraved hieroglyphics that surprise readers of this script who also know German: "So speaks the servant of the king, whose name is the sun and rock of Prussia." And further: "The sovereign lord, the protector of the River Rhine." And so on. That is how Egyptologist Karl Lepsius thanked his patron, King Frederick William IV of Prussia. Nicely done: fawning and sacrilege in equal measure.

478 WHO HAS THE BIGGEST?

Giza / Cholula de Rivadavia. Is the Great Pyramid of Giza the biggest of its type in the world? That depends. If you calculate by height, then at 456 feet (139 meters) it is the winner. But if you take surface area or even volume as the measure, then the Tepanapa Pyramid, close to Cholula de Rivadavia in Mexico, is significantly bigger. Its sides measure 1,476 feet (450 meters) and its volume is over 157 million cubic feet (4.45 million cubic meters), which almost double that of Egypt's Great Pyramid of Giza.

479 LUCKY NEW YORK!

Cairo / New York. If Egyptian viceroy Ismail Pasha had not been so miserly, the New York Statue of Liberty would today be presiding over the Suez Canal. Sculptor Frédéric Auguste Bartholdi (1834–1904) liked his acquaintance's idea of giving the US a symbol of freedom, but he expected more money for it in Cairo. However, there was a lack of money in the Egyptian capital, and "Lady Liberty" made her way to the New World.

480 DELAYED *AIDA*

Suez Canal / Cairo. Contrary to popular belief, the Italian composer Giuseppe Verdi was not commissioned to compose the opera *Aida* for the opening of the Suez Canal. The canal and Cairo's opera house were opened on schedule in 1869 with his *Rigoletto*, albeit that was not its first performance. Cairo hosted the premiere of *Aida* on December 24, 1871, after the costumes and sets had been held up for months in Prussian-besieged Paris during the Franco-Prussian War.

481 THE YEAR HAS THIRTEEN MONTHS

Ethiopia. In this country, the year has thirteen months. The first twelve months have thirty days each, and the thirteenth month has five or six days. It corresponds to the Julian calendar, which is named after Julius Caesar. The majority of the world uses the Gregorian calendar, with twelve months. Thus, Ethiopia is approximately seven years and nine months behind the rest of the world.

482 THE ARK OF THE COVENANT IN ETHIOPIA

Aksum. According to Ethiopian tradition, the Ark of the Covenant, the chest that the Bible says holds the Ten Commandments on two stone slabs, is found in the Church of Our Lady Mary of Zion in the holy city of Aksum. The relic is accessible only for one guardian monk. Although this monk is the only living person to know what this Ethiopian Ark of the Covenant looks like, the country has numerous "copies" for ritual purposes.

483 ALL HAIL HAILE

Shashemene. Ras Tafari ("Prince Tafari") was the shortened name of Emperor of Ethiopia Haile Selassie (1892–1975). In the 1930s, a religious community in Jamaica worshipped him as the reincarnation of the Messiah. The "Rastafarians" are a minority in Jamaica but have spread around the world. Some of them settled in Shashemene in the "promised land" of Ethiopia, when the emperor gave them land in 1948.

484 THE DANCING GOAT THAT DISCOVERED COFFEE

Kaffa. Around 2.5 billion cups of coffee are drunk every day. A goat in the Kingdom of Kaffa is said to be responsible for this coffee consumption. Its shepherd watched it eating a wild coffee bean and then dancing afterward. Kaffa has now long been part of Ethiopia, while coffee went on to become a global indulgence.

485 DON'T SLIP UP

If you make an appointment in Ethiopia, be sure to know whether you are meeting according to Ethiopian or "Western" time. The day begins at twelve (six o'clock in Western time), and in Ethiopia midnight is therefore six o'clock. At home and in many restaurants, it is normal to use your hands and no cutlery to eat. The soft flatbread "replaces" the fork, and you use it to scoop up meat and vegetables. Be sure to wash your hands well before eating!

486 BLISSFUL ISLANDS

Macaronesia. People often get confused by the geography of Macaronesia, believing it is called "Macronesia" and that it is an island archipelago somewhere in the South Seas close to Micronesia. However, that is a mistake: Macaronesia is its correct name, and it means "blessed islands." They are close to Africa in the Atlantic and comprise four archipelagos, from the Azores in the north, southward through Madeira and the Canary Islands, to Cape Verde.

487 THE SAHARA IN THE ATLANTIC

Cape Verde. Geographically speaking, the Cape Verde islands are not part of Africa, since they are more than 186 miles (300 kilometers) from the continental shelf. However, the islands often feel like an outpost of the Sahara when the Harmattan, the strong wind from the desert, blows over them. Sand covers the land that suffers erosion due to goats and wind, and it is prone to drought.

488 FORMER PITSTOP, NOW A VACATION PARADISE

Sal. In the age of steamboats, the Cape Verde islands in the South Atlantic were an important stop on the shipping routes between Europe and South America. They used to stop there to take on coal for the rest of the journey. In the age of air travel before the advent of jets, the islands were also a fuel stop—that is why the former Italian dictator Benito Mussolini had an airport built on the island of Sal. Today, mainly only vacation charter flights land there.

489 A RATHER LAX ATTITUDE TO FAITHFULNESS

Cape Verde. About 98 percent of Cape Verde islanders are Roman Catholic, and consequently there are many churches on the islands. However, they really fill up only on patron saints' days or for funerals, since the islanders are generally not active churchgoers. This stance becomes evident in regard to marriage, which is generally not sealed either religiously or legally. And it is also said that the men of the Cape Verde islands have a very lax interpretation of faithfulness in marriage.

490 DON'T SLIP UP

On the Cape Verde islands, it is considered impolite to eat without offering to share with those around you. Therefore, don't eat on the street or on the bus. If you are invited into someone's home, you can expect that you will be presented with some food, even in the home of a poor family. It is normally the national dish, the *cachupa*, a stew made of corn, beans, vegetables, and chicken or pork if available. A peculiarity of the Cape Verde islanders is their long greetings.

491 A NEW OCEAN FOR KENYA

Kenya. The country is famous for its beaches on the Indian Ocean. Many scientists also believe that the country could soon (maybe in ten million years) also have beaches inland. The reason is the East African Rift, which runs through a large part of the continent and still has volcanic activity. If the rift in the Earth's crust gets deeper, seawater may flood it.

492 A PARK WITH A GATEWAY TO HELL

Hell's Gate National Park. If you are looking for the gateway to hell, try southern Kenya. Hell's Gate was discovered in the nineteenth century by German explorer Gustav Adolf Fischer and is a narrow break in the East African Rift Valley, where the ash from close-by Mount Longonot volcano settled. Hell's Gate is at the bottom of a prehistoric lake, where early humans once lived. The valley and the volcano are separate national parks.

493 FIVE LETTERS—THREE COUNTRIES

Kenya. Guessing Kenya's international country code is not an easy task. Who would think of EAK? That is the abbreviation for East Africa Kenya. The reason for the unusual abbreviation is an agreement between the three East African neighbor states (Kenya, Tanzania, and Uganda) in the East African Community (EAC). Therefore, the abbreviations for Tanzania and Uganda are EAT and EAU, respectively.

494 CAPITAL OF FLAMINGOS AND THIEVES

Nakuru. Kenya's fourth largest city is famous for its alkaline lake of the same name with its countless flamingos. Up to two million of the birds form a pink band around the shallow shore of Lake Nakuru, where they fish for algae and small crabs, which color their feathers. In addition, Nakuru also holds the dubious title of "capital of thieves."

495 MADNESS ON RAILS

Nairobi / Mombasa. The "Lunatic Express" between Nairobi and Mombasa was constructed between 1895 and 1899 by the British colonial government and was given its nickname due to the high costs and the deaths of approximately 1,200 construction workers. In 2017, the 62-mile (100 kilometer) stretch was reopened after a Chinese-financed reconstruction. Today, the trains provide relief for the chronically congested highway between Nairobi and Mombasa.

496 THE WANDERING ISLAND

Madagascar. The island once belonged to two continents. About a hundred million years ago, it broke away from Africa, and about ninety million years ago, it broke away from India. Today, the fourth biggest island in the world lies off the coast of East Africa. During its long isolation, it developed a special collection of fauna. About 80 percent of all the animals here are found only on Madagascar. Hollywood honored this evolution in the animated film *Madagascar*, which has had multiple sequels.

497 UNFAITHFUL ANCESTORS

Madagascar. The heraldic animal of the island is the lemur, one of the primate species that are related to humans. They are treated as holy by many of the island's twenty-two million inhabitants, in the belief that they embody their reincarnated ancestors. Lemurs pick their partners for life. However, the females of the species are notorious for being unfaithful with strong males, thereby optimizing the gene pool. There are around one hundred species of lemur, many of which appear on the list of endangered species.

The lemur is holy in Madagascar (no. 497).

Does this nut look familiar (no. 500)?

498 THE MOST VALUABLE STAMP IN THE WORLD

Mauritius. The island is most famous for the "Blue Mauritius," a rare stamp that was also issued in orange. Both colors generate millions at auctions. The Blue Penny Museum in the capital of Port Louis exhibits both stamps, but only for ten minutes per hour in order to protect them. Sixteen Mauritian companies bought the original stamps at auction in 1993 for $2.2 million.

499 HAVE YOU TRIED THE MILLIONAIRE'S SALAD YET?

Mauritius. There is a culinary myth on Mauritius called "the millionaire's salad." Put more simply, it is a heart-of-palm salad. Heart of palm is the soft bud from which the palm leaves later grow. And there is a rumor that when you remove the heart, the palm tree dies and must be chopped down—and only millionaires can afford that. But then you wonder where all the hearts of palms in the supermarket come from. . .

500 HUMAN ANATOMY IN SEYCHELLES PALMS

Seychelles. Unique to the Seychelles is a legendary palm that bears the largest nut in the world of flora, the coco-de-mer. This nut can weigh up to 99 pounds (45 kilograms) and looks similar to the female lower body, which used to set sailors' fantasies alight. The nut may be exported only with a permit. The male Seychelles palms have inflorescences, which are also associatively really masculine.

501 RECORD BREAKING—AND WITH A SKY VIEW

Casablanca. The Hassan II Mosque in Casablanca, Morocco, was consecrated in 1993. It is only the seventh-biggest Muslim place of worship, but at 690 feet (210 meters), its minarets are higher than any other mosque. And that's not all: it is also the highest tower of a sacred building in the world and beats the highest tower in Christianity, Ulm Minster in Germany, by 165 feet (50 meters). Most of the mosque's roof can be opened up.

502 CASABLANCA WITHOUT CASABLANCA

Casablanca. The world-famous romantic film *Casablanca* was not filmed in the city of Casablanca on account of its budget and the war, instead being almost exclusively filmed in Hollywood studios. But at least the set for Rick's Café was based on the hotel El Minzah in Tangier. In turn, the current Rick's Café in Casablanca was based on the Hollywood set.

503 MOULAY AS A REPLACEMENT MECCA

Moulay Idriss. Morocco's "religious heart," the small town of Moulay Idriss, is barely known to the outside world. It could be because non-Muslims were not permitted to visit it until the twentieth century, because the grave of the state founder Idris I is located within the "holy city." In 788, he brought Islam to Morocco. For poor Moroccans, a pilgrimage to Moulay Idriss can replace the expensive hajj, a pilgrimage to Mecca.

504 NOBLE WOOD

Morocco. In the Atlas Mountains, the Barbary thuja grows. The dashboards of Rolls-Royce cars were once made from its precious wood. In good souvenir shops in Morocco, wares (primarily boxes) made of thuja are sold. However, due to the high price, imitations are also on the market. The Barbary thuja is classed as endangered.

505 DON'T SLIP UP

Where does tipping end and corruption begin in Morocco? Even a large tour operator recommended, "If you are making no progress, then a tip can opens many doors, even doors at the authorities." Morocco is not only geographically the most western land in North Africa, but it is considered culturally the "most Western" Muslim country in Africa. Nevertheless, it is wise to be conservative in religious matters and in regard to women.

506 NOT EIFFEL BUT STILL BEAUTIFUL

Maputo. The biggest train station in Maputo, Mozambique, is considered to be one of the most beautiful in the world and bears the handsome (Portuguese) name Estação dos Caminhos de Ferro de Maputo. Portuguese architects built the station, which opened in 1910. The stucco façade was designed by co-owner Pietro Buffa Buccellato. It is but a legend that Frenchman Gustave Eiffel was the constructor.

507 A TRUE RUST BUCKET

Paris / Maputo. In 1892, Gustave Eiffel designed the "iron house" (*casa de ferro*) in Paris. It was then dismantled and rebuilt in Maputo to serve as the governor's residence. However, it never fulfilled that purpose, because in the tropical climate of Mozambique it was, of course, much too hot inside the metal house. The building now houses several museum offices, and parts of it can be visited. Incidentally, Gustave Eiffel, who also built the Eiffel Tower, never went to Maputo.

508 WALLANDER'S "FATHER" HAS A THEATER HERE

Maputo. If you want to experience productions by Henning Mankell (1948–2015), Maputo is the place to be. The Swedish author of the Wallander series (and of many other novels) was the co-director, author, and occasional stage director at the Teatro Avenida. Thanks to dramatist Mankell, who always spent half the year in his second home in Mozambique, the professional theater group gained international renown.

509 DANCING LIKE TOFO TOFO

Maputo. In Maputo, you can occasionally hear and see the Tofo Tofo Dancers, who were invited to the US by Beyoncé in 2011 to train the pop star's dancers for the "Run the World (Girls)" video. The song and the video were great successes for the singer. The *tofo tofo* group does not take much inspiration from Mozambique's rich dance culture but mixes *kwaito* music and *pantsula* dance, both of which originate from South Africa.

510 DON'T SLIP UP

Religion and churches are generally not a good topic of conversation for foreigners in many countries. That also goes for Mozambique, which is generally religiously tolerant. Special aspects of animism (a spiritual-religious perception of nature) are prevalent there. Even devout Christians and Muslims often follow such rituals, so it is best not to make any negative comments about "heathen faith." In Mozambique, greetings are often excessive, and it is usual to be asked about the health of your family.

511 FASTER THAN A FERRARI

Otjiwarongo. Nowhere in the world is home to more cheetahs than Namibia. An estimated two to three thousand of the big cats live there. They are the fastest animals on land and can reach 68 miles per hour (110 kilometers per hour) in three seconds. Cheetahs are the most endangered big cats in Africa. The Cheetah Conservation Fund does conservation work for the animals.

512 SUNDAY LUNCH IN THE ATLANTIC?

Roastbeef / Plumpudding. It does not get more British than Sunday lunch with roast beef and plum pudding. But the small islands bearing these names are part of the Penguin Islands off the coast of Namibia. Guano (fertilizer from bird droppings) was once harvested there, but the islands are now uninhabited. In contrast to Roastbeef Island (official name: Sinclair), there are two other uninhabited islands called Plumpudding: one in Australia and the other in the Pacific Solomon Islands.

513 THE BIGGEST UNDERGROUND LAKE

Otavi Mountains. The biggest underground lake in the world lies at a depth of 216 feet (66 meters) in the Dragon's Breath Cave. The lake has a surface area of 6.4 acres and is 275 feet (84 meters) deep. The cave was discovered in 1986 and is named after the steam clouds that it occasionally exudes.

514 MYSTERY UNDER WATER

Otjikoto Lake. This sinkhole lake close to the mining town of Tsumeb is at least 246 feet (75 meters) deep. It hides a lot of military equipment that the German colonial troops sunk in 1915, and it is a mystery to researchers. With the exception of Lake Guinas, 9 miles (15 kilometers) away, it is the only lake in Namibia that has water the whole year through. A plausible theory: there could be an underground channel between the lakes, or even running to Etosha National Park.

515 DESERT COAST

Skeleton Coast. The name is truly not inviting, but it is suitable for the coastline in northern Namibia. Although the majority of the "skeletons" come from stranded ships, sometimes bleached whalebones or even skeletons of drowned people wash up. This is where the oldest desert in the world, the Namib Desert (eighty million years old), meets the cold and strong currents of the foggy Atlantic.

516 AN ELEPHANT IN THE HOTEL LOBBY

South Luangwa National Park. Each year in October and November, the Mfuwe Lodge in Zambia greets important guests who test the tiles in the reception area with a staggering 8,800 pounds of weight. Nearly every day, an elephant family strolls through the hotel to get to the wild mango trees in the garden, feasts on them, and then saunters back. That is just how it is if you build a hotel on an elephant path.

517 SWIMMING IN THE DEVIL'S POOL

Victoria Falls. The border between Zambia and Zimbabwe runs through the powerful waterfall. But it is only on the Zambian side that you can experience something magical: a bath directly on the edge of the 328-foot (100 meter) waterfall, in the "Devil's Pool." From September to December, less water flows in the Zambezi River, making it possible to swim from Livingstone Island to the natural pool in the rocks.

518 WATCH OUT, RIVER GOD!

Lake Kariba. In the Zambezi reservoir on the border between Zimbabwe and Zambia, the *Nyaminyami*, a snake monster, is rumored to live. Many of the locals blame the unusual natural catastrophes that occurred during the construction of the Kariba Dam in the 1950s on the anger of the river god because the 420-foot-long (128 meter) wall separated him from his wife. And when the earth quakes in the Zambezi Valley, everyone knows that it is the river god moving.

519 OLD TESTAMENT MISTAKE

Zimbabwe. Zimbabwe was thought to be the country that was called "Ophir" in the Old Testament and whose gold and diamonds made King Solomon endlessly rich. The diamond mines of Cecil Rhodes, who was the namesake of colonial Rhodesia (now known as Zimbabwe), appeared to confirm belief in this theory. However, researchers have now rejected this theory, and the search for Ophir continues.

520 MISS MEDICINE WOMAN

Zimbabwe. Medicine men, called *n'anga* in many countries in Africa, are not folklore in Zimbabwe. Their healing and religious services are still in demand. They have their own professional organization, the Zimbabwe National Traditional Healers Association. A prominent member is Nomusa Ndiweni, a former Miss Zimbabwe, who swapped her career on the catwalk to train as a *n'anga*.

521 THE SPEEDY LAND QUARTET

South Africa. Every safari tourist goes in search of the "Big Five Game" (elephant, lion, leopard, rhinoceros, and buffalo). However, it is less known that you can also observe the four fastest land animals in South Africa. The record holder by far is the cheetah (61 miles per hour). No. 2 is the American pronghorn gazelle (60 miles per hour), followed by the lion (50 miles per hour) and finally the antelopes, including the wildebeest and springboks.

522 THE WRONG CAPE

Cape Town. South Africa's second biggest city is not far from the Cape of Good Hope. Thus, the metropolis uses the slogan "the only city in the world between two oceans." It's a nice saying, but it's sadly incorrect—the Atlantic and Indian Oceans meet approximately 124 miles (200 kilometers) farther southeast at Cape Agulhas, the actual most southerly point of the African mainland.

523 SPECIAL BEDS FOR BEARS AND BEATLES

Cape Town. The Grand Daddy Hotel in Cape Town offers something unique: camping on its roof in one of seven American Airstream caravans, which look like small zeppelins. They all have been designed by local artists. For instance, one known as the "Ballad of John and Yoko" is a Beatles-themed romantic retreat, while the "Goldilocks" van is equipped with costumes (including a bear suit) to reenact the fairy tale.

524 THE BIGGEST DIAMOND HOLE

Kimberley. The Big Hole in Kimberley is a tourist magnet. The 787-foot-deep (240 meter) hole, which is now partially filled with water, has a circumference of 1 mile (1.6 kilometers). Between 1871 and 1914, diamonds weighing more 14.5 million carats were mined from the "deepest man-made mine." Is it really the deepest? Only if you add the qualifier "dug without heavy machinery."

525 DON'T SLIP UP

In South Africa, Western table manners are normal. However, there are exceptions—thanks to a large Asian (predominantly Indian) share of the population. Some meals, for example rice curry dishes, may be eaten without cutlery, from hand to mouth. However, as is usual in Asia and other parts of the world, you use only your right hand. The left hand is considered unclean.

526 LOTS OF LIFE IN THE DORMANT VOLCANO

Ngorongoro. The Ngorongoro Crater on the edge of Tanzania's Serengeti savanna is not only the biggest entirely preserved volcano crater in the world, but it is also home to twenty-five thousand large animals, from elephants to rhinos. Their numbers include the most predators in Africa, particularly lions and leopards.

527 MELTING GLACIERS IN AFRICA

Tanzania. Are there glaciers in Africa? Yes, there still are. They cover only approximately 3.86 square miles (10 square kilometers), and the majority of them are found on the highest mountain on the continent: Mount Kilimanjaro (19,337 feet or 5,895 meters) in Tanzania. They are melting quickly, and scientists predict that they will have completely liquified by 2030.

528 THE THIRTY-EIGHT-MINUTE WAR

Zanzibar. The island is an autonomous region of Tanzania. It lost its independence back in 1896, during the shortest war in world history. The conflict started on August 27 at nine o'clock and ended at 9:38. In the end, a far superior British naval squadron razed a fortress and the sultan's palace.

529 GODFATHERS AND DIVERS

Mafia. Mafia Island (yes, that is its real name) is an island in the Zanzibar Archipelago, which was part of German East Africa during the colonial era. At the time, the name did not attract much attention among the Germans, since the Italian criminal syndicate was unknown. Mafia is a popular mini archipelago for divers, and it has barely been touched by normal tourism due to difficult travel links.

530 DON'T SLIP UP

In rural Tanzania, it is commonplace that men and women eat separately, and it is frowned upon if a foreigner comments on it. Couples who are invited for dinner can offer to adhere to the custom. If you are asked whether you would like an alcoholic beverage, your best bet is local beer, because Tanzanian wine is generally very sweet. Even though the same can be said for *Afrikoko*, a chocolate and coconut milk liqueur, it is worth trying it with local coffee or tea.

531 ONCE A HAREM, NOW A MUSEUM

Tunis. The National Museum of Tunisia has found a good home in the former harem of Bardo Palace in Tunis. Not much evidence is left of the former use of the building, even though such women's quarters belonging to exotic rulers inspired the fantasies of many European artists. The museum houses the best archeological collection in North Africa with a focus on Roman artifacts.

532 PRESIDENT OF GRANDEUR

Monastir. During his lifetime, Tunisia's first president, Habib Bourguiba (1903–2000), had a large mausoleum constructed (and a mosque named after him) in his city of birth. The tomb is a beautiful example of Arabic architecture, and the large square belonging to it is a popular meeting point.

533 MONTY PYTHON'S FILM SET

Monastir. The biggest (also in terms of size) attraction in Monastir is the ribat, which was built in 769 and is one of the oldest fortresses in North Africa. Cinema enthusiasts will recognize the fort; it was used as one of the settings in Franco Zeffirelli's biblical film *Jesus of Nazareth* (1977). The British Monty Python troupe also used the ribat two years later for their controversial Jesus comedy *Life of Brian*.

534 FROM EMPEROR TO KING

Tunis / Carthage. In the garden of the National Museum of Carthage, there is a 10-foot (3 meter) marble statue. It is claimed to be a likeness of French king Louis IX, who died in 1270 during the siege of neighboring Tunis. Presumably, the artist did not know what he looked like, because he simply copied a statue of Emperor Charles V. Carthage cathedral on the Byrsa Hill is also named after King Louis.

535 BABIES SACRIFICED FOR BAAL

Tunis / Carthage. Appropriately for a temple to the "weather god" Baal, the ruins of the Tophet in Carthage are situated in the sun. However, they may be hiding a dark secret: Were the firstborn babies once sacrificed here? Some researchers who investigated the buried urns believe that to be the case. A different theory is that the urns contain the ashes of children who died of natural causes shortly after birth.

536 EVERYTHING FLOWS IN GAMBIA

The Gambia. On the map, the Gambia, Africa's smallest state in terms of land, looks like a colon that reaches from the southern Atlantic coast into the territory of much larger Senegal. This unusual border follows the winding path of the Gambia River. The country's borders on either side of the riverbanks are generally just 6 to 9 miles (10 to 15 kilometers) away. That is how far the cannons of the British river cruisers could fire in colonial times.

537 PREGNANT THROUGH THE POWER OF CROCODILES

The Gambia. In popular belief, crocodiles are holy. For that reason and because water is said to have magical powers, the three pools where Nile crocodiles are kept have become a place of pilgrimage for Gambian brides wanting to ensure a fertile marriage or for women who are struggling to get pregnant. Stroking the reptiles on land is said to also bring luck.

538 MISUNDERSTANDING WITH CONSEQUENCES

Abidjan. Like many place names in former colonies, the name of Abidjan, the old capital city of the Ivory Coast, is a result of a misunderstanding between the Europeans and the locals. A Portuguese or Frenchman is said to have asked locals who came out of the forest with bundles of twigs where the nearest town was. But they answered, "We come from cutting leaves," in Bantu (*t'chan m'bi djan*). And from that, the name Abidjan arose.

539 ALL ROADS LEAD TO YAMOUSSOUKRO

Yamoussoukro. Where is the biggest Christian church? St. Peter's Basilica in Rome, of course. Actually, no—even if the pope doesn't like it. The biggest church in Christendom, the Basilica of Our Lady of Peace, is in the capital city of the Ivory Coast, Yamoussoukro. It is built over a surface area of 320,000 square feet (30,000 square meters), and it is also 85 feet (26 meters) higher than its competitor.

540 DON'T SLIP UP

Teranga, the culture of sharing, is very important in Senegal. If you have something to eat, you offer it to others, even if they often say no. If you get to know the Senegalese beyond simple tourist exchanges, you should be acquainted with the "principle of Teranga." It also stands for hospitality or religious tolerance. Often Muslims will celebrate Christmas with Christians, who in turn break the fast with their neighbors. *Teranga* could also be a synonym for Senegal, and the soccer team even calls itself "the lions of Teranga."

Church worship in the Antarctic at the Russian Orthodox Trinity Church (no. 541).

541 NO GOD IN THE ANTARCTIC?

Antarctica. "Below 40 degrees south there is no law. Below 50 degrees south there is no God." This famous quote about the Antarctic is no longer true. Today, there are seven churches on the seventh continent, from the Chapel of the Snows (1956) on the US McMurdo station to the Russian Orthodox Trinity Church (2004). They have performed marriages and even baptisms. Cruise ship passengers have also attended services in the deepest South.

542 WAFERS INSTEAD OF WEAPONS

Antarctica. If you follow the Antarctic trails, you can take a history-laden picnic with you: Necco® wafers from the US. The colorful treat, which has been produced since 1847, accompanied Richard E. Byrd in 1933 on his second Antarctic expedition. The admiral had a 2.5-ton stash of them; over the course of two years, his team consumed a pound each week. Since then, the wafers have been iconic in the United States.

543 UNA'S BREASTS IN ICE

Antarctica. The Lemaire Channel, between the Antarctic peninsula and an island, not only is one of the most beautiful straits in this world of ice but also has a bit of a racy history. At the entrance to the channel, there is a double summit called Una Peaks. However, the unofficial name is older: Una's Tits. The name refers to Una Spivey, who worked for an Antarctica organization.

544 DON'T FORGET YOUR SWIMSUIT

Antarctica. Want to go swimming in the sea? In the Antarctic? We recommend Deception Island. It is a half-submerged volcano into whose caldera ships can sail. At a place close to the shore, near an old whaling station, a hot spring bubbles into the cold sea. This is where cruise ship crews often dig out a "bath" in the volcanic sand for the passengers to pose in pleasantly warm water for the obligatory photos.

545 DON'T SLIP UP

The rule book is particularly important in Antarctica because it conserves the fragile environment. That means not stepping on the rare plants in ice-free zones, since otherwise they would need years to recover on the driest continent in the world. There is also a rule about keeping 16 feet (5 meters) of distance from animals. At this latitude, "animals" generally means penguins of various species. Since the birds are curious, sometimes they do not observe the 16-feet rule themselves.

546 BOOZING IN THE FOREST?

The Arctic. "Drunken forests": Do they really exist? Yes, they can be found on the Arctic treeline in Alaska, Canada, and Siberia. The trees in these forests look like staggering drunks, chaotically leaning in all directions. They are growing in the permafrost zones, which briefly thawed. In the boggy ground, the trees have less support, and when the earth freezes again, the trees remain in the new position.

547 VOCABULARY MYTH

The Arctic. The Inuit have four hundred words for "snow." This claim is ever present in reports about the Arctic, but it is not correct, as proven by Geoffrey K. Pullum, professor of general linguistics at the University of Edinburgh. The number refers back to a text that is over one hundred years old. In actual fact, the Inuit have at most a couple of dozen words for snow.

548 WEAPONS IN THE COCKPIT

The Arctic. In the 1960s, new jet planes made air routes from Europe to Asia possible. Because of the shape of planet Earth, they flew over the North Pole to Alaska and then continued over the Pacific after a fuel stop. In 1964, when Lufthansa flew this route to Tokyo, the pilots were prepared for an emergency landing on the polar ice and were equipped with snowshoes, bright red down snowsuits, a snow saw to build an igloo, and shotguns to ward off polar bears.

Thanks to a hot spring, you can swim on Deception Island in Antarctica (no. 544).

549 WHAT IS THAT WHITE STUFF?

The Arctic. The Siberian tiger is the biggest cat in the world and is also one of the most endangered. There are only around five hundred of them living in the wild and four hundred in zoos around the world, with many of them having been born in captivity. In 1995, the British *Daily Express* newspaper reported that the zoo on the Isle of Wight had to acquaint its tigers with snow when they saw it for the first time.

550 WHERE CAN YOU FIND RED GOLF BALLS?

Uummannaq. The "greens" are "whites" and the balls are red at the World Ice Golf Championship, which takes place in mid-March in Uummannaq in Greenland. Clubs with graphite shafts are not recommended, because they could split in the cold. Golfers with a handicap of at least thirty-six can register to participate in the two-day competition. Thirty-six holes are played on the nine-hole course on a frozen fjord. Each year, the golf course is remade.

551 CHECK-IN AT THE SPACE INN

Moon. Tourists have already been to space. Now travel companies, such as the one owned by billionaire Richard Branson, are also wanting to offer flights to the moon—with stopovers in spaceship hotels. They should be able to comfortably break up the long journey to the moon, which incidentally gets longer each year. The moon moves a little more than 2 inches (6 centimeters) farther away from Earth each year.

552 MONUMENT IN DUST

Moon. There is not quite enough to see yet for an art tour, but there is already one monument on the moon. *Fallen Astronaut* is a 3.5-inch aluminum figure that lies in the dust. The work by Belgian artist Paul Van Hoeydonck was taken to the moon in 1971 by David Scott. It is accompanied by a plaque with the names of all astronauts who had died in service until that point. At the time, two additional names were being kept secret by the Soviet Union.

553 MOON BOOTS IN SIZE 9½

Moon. There is not (yet) a souvenir shop on the moon. But how would you like the boots that Neil Armstrong wore in 1969, when—as the first man on the moon—he said, "That's one small step for man, one giant leap for mankind"? The contaminated moon boots were left behind and did not make the return flight to the Apollo 11 spaceship. The boots are size US 9½.

554 WEIGHTLESS EXERCISE

Moon. Playing sports on the moon? It will be no problem for future space tourists. They need to pack only a six-iron golf club, because there are already two golf balls up there. They were hit by Alan Shepard, who was the first American in space and later became the fifth man on the moon in 1971. There is also a "javelin" (a pole for a solar test) up there that was thrown by his partner and lunar module pilot, Edgar D. Mitchell.

555 GALACTIC NATIONAL PARK

Moon. The US wants to create a national park to protect its historic places on the moon, such as the landing site of the Apollo missions and Neil Armstrong's famous footprints. A draft of a corresponding law for this purpose has already been proposed. Other nations regard this proposition with skepticism, referencing the UN Outer Space Treaty. So, for the time being, Americans will have to content themselves with the Craters of the Moon National Monument in Idaho.

Is the moon suitable as a tourist destination? Only time will tell (nos. 551–555).

Library of Congress Control Number: 2022932587

Author: Klaus Viedebantt
Product manager: Susanne Kaufmann
Editor: Mareike Weber
Layout: Elke Made
Illustration: Frank Duffek
Cover design: Chris Bower
Front cover image inspiration: Misha Sotnikov/Bigstock.com
Back cover image: coboflupi/Bigstock.com

All information in this book has been carefully researched and updated by the author and has been checked by the publishing house. However, we can accept no liability for the information being correct, and you use this book at your own risk.

Image credits:
Picture Alliance: pp. 4 (Karl-Heinz Ei), 6–7 (Photoshoot), 11 (maxppp), 20–21, 25, 57, 122, 128, 146–147, 190–191 (dpa), 30–31 (Design Pics), 33, 107 (landov), 42–43 (ANP Kippa), 60 (akg-images), 112–113, 126–127 (Bildagentur-o), 150–151 (WILDLIFE), 155 (Arco Images G), 158–159 (Robert Harding World Imagery), 170 (Artcolor), 182–183 (Robert Harding World Imagery), 186–187 (K. Wothe);

Shutterstock: pp. 64–65 (Markus Mainka), 78–78 (Matt9122), 89 (Klemen Misic), 91 (Elzbieta Sekowska), 94–95 (Manamana), 102–103 (irisphoto1), 110 (Zhukov Oleg), 162–163 (Anna Omelchenko), 169 (Ronald Ijdema), 189 (Aphelleon), illustrations for Fall, Summer Solstice (AVIcon), illustrations for Easter (Visual Generation), illustration for Christmas (Fine Art);

Jan Beuell: p.15

Type set in Veneer Two/Frutiger LT 45 Light

ISBN: 978-0-7643-6505-8

Printed in India

Published by Schiffer Publishing, Ltd.
4880 Lower Valley Road
Atglen, PA 19310
Phone: (610) 593-1777; Fax: (610) 593-2002
Email: Info@schifferbooks.com
Web: www.schifferbooks.com

Schiffer Publishing's titles are available at special discounts for bulk purchases for sales promotions or premiums. Special editions, including personalized covers, corporate imprints, and excerpts, can be created in large quantities for special needs. For more information, contact the publisher.

A somewhat different round of golf on Greenland. Here the balls are red (no. 550).